New Paris Interiors
Nouveaux intérieurs parisiens

New Paris Interiors

Nouveaux intérieurs parisiens

Edited by | Sous la direction de | Herausgegeben von
Angelika Taschen

Text by | Text de | Text von
Ian Phillips

TASCHEN

HONG KONG KÖLN LONDON LOS ANGELES MADRID PARIS TOKYO

Endpapers | Pages de garde | Vorsatz :
The building on Square des Batignolles, which houses the flat of musician Bertrand Burgalat, is
typical of the Haussmann style. | L'immeuble typiquement haussmannien du musicien Bertrand
Burgalat, près du Square des Batignolles. | Das Gebäude an der Square des Batignolles, in dem
sich die Wohnung des Musikers Bertrand Burgalat befindet, ist typisch für den Haussmann-Stil.

Despite intensive research it has not always been possible to establish copyright
ownership. Where this is the case we would appreciate notification.

© 2008 TASCHEN GmbH
Hohenzollernring 53, D–50672 Köln
www.taschen.com

© 2008 VG Bild-Kunst, Bonn for the works of André Arbus, Jean-Michel Basquiat,
Harry Bertoia, Max Bill, Alighiero Boetti, Christian Boltanski, Daniele Buetti,
René Collamarini, Bernard Dufour, Thomas Fougeirol, Gérard Garouste,
Alberto Giacometti, Fabrice Hyber, Claude Lalanne, Ange Leccia, Hubert Le Gall,
Roy Lichtenstein, René Magritte, Mathieu Matégot, Philippe Meste, François Morellet,
Jean-Michel Othoniel, Charlotte Perriand, Christian de Portzamparc, Pierre Pozzi,
Jean Prouvé, Germaine Richier, Axel Salto, Alain Séchas, Roger Tallon, Xavier Veilhan,
Erwin Wurm and Chen Zhen.
© 2008 FLC/VG Bild-Kunst, Bonn for the works of Le Corbusier.
© 2008 for the work of Andreas Gursky,
courtesy: Monika Sprüth/Philomene Magers/VG Bild-Kunst, Bonn
© 2008 The Isamu Noguchi Foundation and Garden Museum/VG Bild-Kunst,
Bonn for the works of Isamu Noguchi.
© 2008 for the works of Charles and Ray Eames: Eames Office, Venice, CA,
www.eamesoffice.com.
© 2008 Takashi Murakami/Kaikai Kiki Co, Ltd. All rights reserved.

Compilation, editing & layout: Angelika Taschen, Berlin
General Project Manager: Stephanie Bischoff, Cologne
Text: Ian Phillips, Paris
Special contributor: Mathieu Paris, Paris
French translation: Philippe Safavi, Paris
German translation: Christiane Burkhart, textkontor, Munich
Production: Thomas Grell, Cologne

Printed in China
ISBN 978-3-8365-0250-4
ISBN 978-3-8365-0252-8 (edition with French cover)

Contents
Sommaire
Inhalt

Paris revisited
Preface by Angelika Taschen

Paris revisité
Préface de Angelika Taschen

Paris revisited
Vorwort von Angelika Taschen

It is exactly 15 years since I edited the first "Paris Interiors" volume. The book marked the beginning of a new series that was an immediate success. Paris was followed by Morocco, London, New York, Berlin, Provence and many more. There are devoted collectors all over the world who proudly tell me they have bought all the volumes in the series. And it makes me very happy every time I hear how much these books have inspired them.

"Paris" has in the meantime enjoyed a short beauty sleep and is now ready to present itself with new élan. On the other hand, since 1992, technology has developed with breathtaking speed. How well I remember, for the original Paris book and the subsequent volumes, having to make a paltry brownish colour photocopy of each individual slide I had chosen for the layout. Once the precise percentage of the enlargement had been calculated, it took a couple of minutes for the copying machine to print the four colors one after the other. Then I had to trim the copy by hand, push it through a wax machine and glue it to the printed sheet – only to realise that the result did not quite meet my expectations. And so the nerve-racking procedure started all over again with a new photograph.

I still ask myself sometimes how I managed to produce books then, books that can even be reprinted today and looked at without embarrassment. Now I receive digital scans by computer, which I can insert into the layout in a matter of fractions of a second. If the result is not to my liking, I can try five or six alternative motifs at lightning speed – until I am one hundred percent satisfied.

But not only has technology progressed. A new generation of photographers, designers and architects has emerged whose works are shaping the appearance of the new millennium. Art and design are increasingly merging, and are almost eye to eye. Today there are galleries not only for art, but also for contemporary design. The most important art fairs are complemented by design fairs, and the exorbitant prices of designer furniture are often very close to those of artworks. And there seems to be no end in sight to this development.

Voilà juste quinze ans que j'ai publié « Paris Interiors », le premier ouvrage d'une collection dont le succès ne s'est pas fait attendre. Il a été suivi de livres sur le Maroc, Londres, New York, Berlin, la Provence et bien d'autres encore. Des collectionneurs passionnés de tous les coins du monde me racontent avec fierté qu'ils les ont tous achetés. Quand ils m'avouent ensuite combien ces livres les ont inspirés, je suis ravie.

Pendant ce temps, Paris s'est refait une beauté pour se présenter aujourd'hui plus vivante que jamais. Et puis la technologie s'est développée à une vitesse vertigineuse depuis 1992. Je me souviens encore très bien du livre sur Paris et des ouvrages suivants : je devais faire une copie en couleur – brunâtre et boueuse – de chaque diapositive choisie pour la maquette.

Il fallait calculer exactement le pourcentage de l'agrandissement et attendre la copieuse qui mettait plusieurs minutes à appliquer les quatre couleurs l'une après l'autre. Ensuite il fallait découper la copie à la main, la glisser dans une machine à cirer et la coller sur l'épreuve – et tout cela pour me rendre compte que le résultat ne me plaisait pas. Je choisissais alors une autre photo et la procédure énervante recommençait de plus belle.

Je me demande encore comment j'ai réussi à faire des livres que l'on puisse aujourd'hui réimprimer et regarder sans rougir. Il n'y a pas si longtemps que j'obtiens, grâce à l'ordinateur, des scans numériques que je peux insérer dans la maquette en une fraction de seconde. Si le résultat ne me plaît pas, je retente le coup très vite avec cinq ou six autres motifs – jusqu'à ce que je sois absolument satisfaite.

Mais la technologie n'est pas la seule à avoir évolué. Une nouvelle génération de photographes, de designers et d'architectes occupent le devant de la scène et leurs travaux marquent de leur empreinte le visage du nouveau millénaire. L'art et le design fusionnent de plus en plus et se trouvent presque à hauteur d'yeux. Ainsi on voit aujourd'hui à côté des galeries d'art des galeries consacrées au design contemporain. Les principales foires de l'art sont complétées par des foires du design, et les prix exorbitants qu'atteignent les meubles design n'ont

Genau 15 Jahre sind vergangen, seit ich den ersten Band »Paris Interiors« herausgegeben habe. Das Buch war der Auftakt einer neuen Reihe, die sofort sehr erfolgreich war. Es folgten Bände über Marokko, London, New York, Berlin, die Provence und viele weitere. Überall auf der Welt gibt es leidenschaftliche Sammler, die mir stolz erzählen, alle Bände der Reihe gekauft zu haben. Wenn ich dann noch höre, wie sehr sie diese Bücher inspiriert haben, macht mich das jedes Mal sehr glücklich.

In der Zwischenzeit hat Paris einen kleinen Schönheitsschlaf gehalten, um heute wieder mit neuer Lebendigkeit aufzuwarten. Dafür hat sich die Technik seit 1992 mit atemberaubendem Tempo weiterentwickelt. Ich kann mich noch sehr genau erinnern, wie ich damals für das Paris-Buch und die folgenden Bände von jedem einzelnen Dia, das ich für das Layout ausgesucht hatte, eine schmuddelige, braunsoßige Farbkopie machen musste. Nachdem ich zuvor genauestens die Prozentzahl der Vergrößerung ausgerechnet hatte, dauerte es Minuten, bis der Kopierer die vier Farben nacheinander auftrug. Anschließend musste die Kopie von Hand ausgeschnitten, durch eine Wachsmaschine geschoben und auf den Satzbogen geklebt werden – nur um dann festzustellen, dass das Ergebnis meinen Ansprüchen nicht genügte. Also ging die nervenzehrende Prozedur mit einem neuen Foto von vorne los.

Ich frage mich immer noch, wie ich damals die Bücher so hinbekommen habe, dass man sie heute noch nachdrucken und, ohne in Verlegenheit zu geraten, anschauen kann. Seit nicht so langer Zeit erhalte ich via Computer digitale Scans, die ich in Bruchteilen einer Sekunde in das Layout einfügen kann. Gefällt mir das Resultat nicht, probiere ich in Windeseile fünf, sechs alternative Motive aus – bis ich hundertprozentig zufrieden bin.

Aber nicht nur die Technik hat sich entwickelt. Es ist eine neue Generation von Fotografen, Designern und Architekten herangewachsen, die mit ihren Arbeiten das Gesicht des neuen Jahrtausends prägen. Kunst und Design wachsen immer enger zusammen und befinden sich fast auf Augenhöhe. So gibt es heute nicht nur Galerien für Kunst, sondern auch für zeitgenössisches Design. Die wichtigen Kunst-

It is no coincidence that today some of the world's most renowned designers and gallery owners again have their headquarters in Paris. After all, it is home to an elegant and financially solvent clientele and to ardent collectors with impeccable taste.

Interior designers in Paris work closely with design galleries, thus ensuring an appropriate setting for the valuable items. This gives rise to enchanting presentations of a calibre achieved nowhere else in the world.

Now that French designers like Jean Prouvé, Charlotte Perriand and Jean Royère are regarded as classics worldwide, a new international generation is setting the tone in Paris – like the Bouroullec brothers, Martin Szekely, Marc Newson and India Mahdavi.

The marvellous thing about Paris is that despite globalisation the city radiates its very own charm, in art and designs as in other fields, and succeeds in remaining incomparable and romantic. Among the reasons for this are the fact that people here work not against, but with tradition.

For me it was certainly a great pleasure to discover and assemble the wonderful and extraordinary apartments presented in this book. I would like to express my gratitude to all the residents, photographers, journalists, gallery owners and designers who helped me to capture 21st-century Paris. And to repeat it yet again: Paris est très, très chic!

souvent plus rien à envier à ceux des œuvres d'art. La fin de cette évolution n'est pas prévisible.

Le fait que quelques-uns des designers et des galeries les plus renommés sur la scène internationale ont de nouveau pignon sur rue à Paris n'a rien d'étonnant : c'est ici aussi que vivent des clients élégants et solvables, des collectionneurs passionnés au goût sûr.

Les designers d'intérieur parisiens collaborent étroitement avec des galeries de design, ce qui leur permet d'assurer la présentation adéquate des précieux objets. Une magie de la mise en scène voit ainsi le jour que l'on ne trouve nulle part ailleurs.

Alors que des designers français comme Jean Prouvé, Charlotte Perriand et Jean Royère sont considérés aujourd'hui comme des classiques, une nouvelle génération internationale donne le ton de nos jours à Paris – nous ne citerons que les frères Bouroullec, Martin Szekely, Marc Newson et India Mahdavi.

Le miracle, c'est qu'en dépit de la mondialisation qui se fait sentir aussi dans les domaines de l'art et du design, Paris n'a rien perdu de son charme très particulier et reste inégalable et romantique. Cela tient aussi au fait que l'on ne travaille pas contre la tradition ici mais avec elle.

Moi en tout cas, j'ai eu beaucoup de plaisir à découvrir et rassembler les habitations merveilleuses et sortant de l'ordinaire présentées dans ce livre. Je remercie leurs occupants ainsi que les photographes, les journalistes, les galeristes et les designers qui m'ont aidée à saisir le Paris du XXIᵉ siècle. Je ne peux que le répéter : Paris est très, très chic !

messen werden von Designmessen ergänzt, und die exorbitanten Preise für Designmöbel stehen denen für Kunstwerke oft nicht mehr nach. Ein Ende dieser Entwicklung ist nicht absehbar.

Es ist kein Zufall, dass heute einige der weltweit renommiertesten Designer und Galerien ihren Sitz wieder in Paris haben, denn hier leben eine elegante, zahlungskräftige Klientel und passionierte Sammler mit erlesenem Geschmack.

Die Pariser Interiordesigner arbeiten eng mit Designgalerien zusammen und sorgen so für eine angemessene Präsentation der kostbaren Stücke. Auf diese Weise entsteht eine Magie der Inszenierung, die auf der Welt ohne Beispiel ist.

Nachdem französische Designer wie Jean Prouvé, Charlotte Perriand und Jean Royère inzwischen weltweit zu den Klassikern zählen, gibt in Paris heute eine neue internationale Generation den Ton an – so wie die Brüder Bouroullec, Martin Szekely, Marc Newson und India Mahdavi.

Das große Wunder von Paris ist, dass die Stadt trotz Globalisierung auch auf den Gebieten der Kunst und des Designs ihren höchst eigenen Charme und Flair verbreitet und es schafft, unverwechselbar und romantisch zu bleiben. Das liegt auch daran, dass hier nicht gegen die Tradition, sondern mit ihr gearbeitet wird.

Mir jedenfalls hat es sehr große Freude gemacht, die in diesem Buch präsentierten wunderbaren und außergewöhnlichen Wohnungen zu entdecken und zusammenzutragen. Ich danke all den Bewohnern, Fotografen, Journalisten, Galeristen und Designern, die mir geholfen haben, das Paris des 21. Jahrhunderts einzufangen. Noch immer und immer wieder: Paris est très, très chic!

This apartment in the 16th arrondissement certainly has a lot going for it: a 140-square-metre roof garden, views of the Eiffel Tower and a spectacular double-height main room. It was originally constructed around a number of architectural elements. In the wood-panelled sitting room are a stained-glass window and vintage Versailles parquet. In the main room, an imposing oak fireplace carved with lion's heads, a 19th-century balustrade and 15th-century pillars. Architect Christian Baquiast's mandate was to open up the space. He created an aperture above the fireplace and bestowed the master bedroom with a porthole. He also paid homage to the flat's architectural heritage. "My idea," he says, "was to use industrial materials, but to give them a classical twist." An example? A concrete wall bearing a wood-grain relief, created using a mould of an oak plank.

Rue des Belles-Feuilles

Cet appartement du 16ᵉ arrondissement a tout pour lui : un jardin en terrasse de 140 mètres carrés, des vues sur la Tour Eiffel et un séjour spectaculaire avec double hauteur sous plafond. Il a été construit autour d'éléments architecturaux. Le petit salon lambrissé possède un vitrail et un parquet Versailles ; le living, une imposante cheminée en chêne sculptée de têtes de lion, une balustrade du XIXᵉ siècle et des poutres du XVᵉ. L'architecte Christian Baquiast avait pour consigne d'ouvrir l'espace. Il a créé une ouverture au-dessus de la cheminée et un hublot dans la chambre principale, respectant le patrimoine architectural des lieux. « J'ai voulu utiliser des matériaux industriels en leur donnant une tournure classique », explique-t-il. Exemple : un mur en béton texturé imitant le grain du bois, réalisé à l'aide du moulage d'une planche en chêne.

Dieses Appartement im 16. Arrondissement hat wirklich einiges zu bieten, unter anderem einen 140 Quadratmeter großen Dachgarten mit Blick auf den Eiffelturm und einen spektakulär hohen Raum mit Galerie. Ursprünglich wurde es um mehrere Architekturelemente herumgebaut. Im holzvertäfelten Wohnzimmer gibt es ein Buntglasfenster sowie altes Versailles-Parkett. Im großen Wohnraum befinden sich ein imposanter Eichenkamin mit geschnitzten Löwenköpfen, ein Geländer aus dem 19. Jahrhundert sowie Säulen aus dem 15. Jahrhundert. Die Aufgabe des Architekten Christian Baquiast bestand darin, die Räume zu verbinden. Er sorgte für eine Öffnung über dem Kamin und bestückte das Schlafzimmer mit einem Bullauge. Trotzdem respektierte er das architektonische Erbe der Wohnung. »Meine Idee war, Industriematerialien zu benutzen, ihnen aber einen klassischen Dreh zu geben.« Ein Beispiel? Die wie Holz gemaserte Betonwand, für die ein Eichenbrett abgegossen wurde.

Below: Baquiast punched a porthole into one wall of the master bedroom.
Following pages: In the wood-panelled sitting room, Jean Royère's "Œuf" sofa and chairs still have their original 1950s fabric. The coffee table is by Olivier Mourgue and the photo a collaboration between Bruno Bressolin and Bruno Juminer. The garden on the terrace was created by landscape architect Hugues Peuvergne.

En bas : Baquiast a percé un hublot dans un mur de la chambre principale.
Pages suivantes : Dans le salon lambrissé, le canapé et les fauteuils « Œuf » de Jean Royère possèdent encore leur tissu d'origine. La table basse est d'Olivier Mourgue. La photo est une œuvre conjointe de Bruno Bressolin et de Bruno Juminer. Le jardin en terrasse a été paysagé par Hugues Peuvergne.

Unten: Baquiast ließ ein Bullauge in eine Schlafzimmerwand brechen.
Folgende Seiten: Das »Œuf«-Sofa und die dazugehörigen Sessel von Jean Royère haben immer noch ihren Originalbezug aus den 1950er-Jahren. Der Couchtisch ist von Olivier Mourgue und das Foto eine Gemeinschaftsarbeit von Bruno Bressolin und Bruno Juminer. Den Garten auf der Dachterrasse schuf der Landschaftsarchitekt Hugues Peuvergne.

Previous pages and facing page: The main room is structured around a 19th-century fireplace. The two copper and glass chandeliers are one-off creations by André Dubreuil. The dining table is by Warren Platner and the two black armchairs by Ignazio Gardella.
Above: The wooden balustrade, which rings the gallery, dates from the 19th century.

Pages précédentes et page de gauche : La pièce principale s'articule autour d'une cheminée du XIXᵉ siècle. Les deux lustres en cuivre et verre sont des pièces uniques signées André Dubreuil. La table de salle à manger est de Warren Platner et les deux fauteuils noirs d'Ignazio Gardella.
En haut : La balustrade en bois de la galerie date du XIXᵉ siècle.

Vorhergehende Seiten und gegenüberliegende Seite: Der Galerieraum ist um einen Kamin aus dem 19. Jahrhundert angeordnet. Die beiden Kronleuchter aus Kupfer und Glas sind Unikate von André Dubreuil. Der Esstisch ist von Warren Platner, und die beiden schwarzen Sessel hat Ignazio Gardella entworfen.
Oben: Das Holzgeländer der Galerie stammt aus dem 19. Jahrhundert.

"It's essentially an apartment for the mind," states interior designer Valérie Mazérat. "The idea was to have pure forms to create a serene atmosphere for thinking." The owner, Maria Bonnafous-Boucher, does a lot of the latter. As an academic, she requested lots of different tables throughout where she could read and write. The ground-floor flat itself is fundamentally classical and Mazérat's approach was to keep that spirit, but update it. Thus, she encased the traditional fireplace with a minimalist surround and painted the vintage parquet in the master bedroom white. She also left the windows without curtains in order to capture as much natural light as possible. The result is certainly very peaceful.

Maria Bonnafous-Boucher

« C'est avant tout un appartement pour l'esprit » explique la décoratrice Valérie Mazérat. « Les formes sont épurées pour avoir une atmosphère sereine propice à la réflexion. » C'est que la propriétaire, l'universitaire Maria Bonnafous-Boucher, est une tête. Elle a demandé à avoir partout des tables sur lesquelles lire et écrire. Situé au-rez-de-chaussée, l'appartement est d'une facture classique que Mazérat a cherché à conserver tout en la modernisant. Elle a enveloppé la cheminée traditionnelle d'un manteau minimaliste, peint en blanc le parquet ancien de la chambre principale et laissé les fenêtres sans rideaux pour laisser entrer le plus de lumière naturelle possible. Le résultat est d'une paix absolue.

»Es ist im Grunde genommen eine Wohnung für den Geist«, sagt die Interiordesignerin Valérie Mazérat. »Es kam mir auf klare Formen an, die eine ruhige Atmosphäre zum Nachdenken schaffen.« Und die Besitzerin, Maria Bonnafous-Boucher, denkt viel nach. Die Akademikerin bat um viele verschiedene Tische, an denen sie lesen und schreiben kann. Die Parterrewohnung ist ein klassischer Pariser Altbau. Mazérat wollte das Klassische erhalten, dem Ganzen aber einen zeitgenössischen Touch verleihen. Deshalb umgab sie den traditionellen Kamin mit einer minimalistischen Einfassung und strich das alte Parkett im Schlafzimmer weiß. Außerdem beließ sie die Fenster ohne Vorhänge, um so viel natürliches Tageslicht hereinzulassen wie möglich. Die Atmosphäre ist vor allem sehr beruhigend. Wie Mazérat sagt: »Es ist weit davon entfernt, das Klischee eines chaotischen Schriftstellers zu erfüllen.«

Previous pages: *A chair by Julian Mayor stands next to an Empire side table and India Mahdavi's "Big Swing" lamp in one corner of the sitting room.*
Above: *The lacquered kitchen units were custom-made.*
Right: *The Corian kitchen table is only one of the places where the owner can read and write.*

Pages précédentes : *Dans un coin du salon, une chaise de Julian Mayor près d'un guéridon Empire et d'un lampadaire « Big Swing » d'India Mahdavi.*
En haut : *Les placards laqués de la cuisine ont été réalisés sur mesure.*
À droite : *La table de cuisine en Corian n'est que l'un des nombreux endroits où la propriétaire aime s'installer pour lire et travailler.*

Vorhergehende Seiten: *Ein Stuhl von Julian Mayor steht neben einem Beistelltischchen im Empire-Stil und der Stehlampe »Big Swing« von India Mahdavi.*
Oben: *Die eingebaute, weiß lackierte Küche ist eine Maßanfertigung.*
Rechts: *Der Küchentisch aus Corian ist nur einer von vielen Plätzen, an denen die Wohnungsbesitzerin schreiben und lesen kann.*

Right: *A view from the kitchen towards a cupboard made from hemlock.*
Below: *For the entrance hall, India Mahdavi created a chest on which the owner can display works of art.*
Following pages: *Contemporary meets classic in the sitting room. Sycamore banquettes by India Mahdavi stand on either side of the fireplace. The Napoleon III armchairs were reupholstered in linen.*

À droite : *Depuis la cuisine, une vue sur un placard en pruche.*
En bas : *Pour le hall d'entrée, India Mahdavi a créé un meuble de rangement sur lequel la propriétaire peut exposer des œuvres d'art.*
Pages suivantes : *Dans le salon, le contemporain côtoie le classique. De chaque côté de la cheminée, des banquettes en sycomore d'India Mahdavi. Les fauteuils Napoléon III ont été retapissés en lin.*

Rechts: *Blick aus der Küche auf einen Schrank aus Kiefernholz.*
Unten: *Für den Flur schuf India Mahdavi ein maßgefertigtes Sideboard, auf dem die Bewohnerin Kunstwerke ausstellen kann.*
Folgende Seiten: *Im Wohnzimmer trifft zeitgenössisches auf klassisches Design. Von India Mahdavi maßgefertigte Bänke aus Platanenholz stehen zu beiden Seiten des Kamins. Die Sessel aus der Napoléon-III-Epoche wurden mit Leinen bezogen.*

Right: *Both the bathroom sink and tap are from Boffi. The cupboards are made of hemlock.*
Below: *The pièce de résistance in the sitting room is an immense sycamore desk custom-designed by Mahdavi.*

À droite : *Le lavabo et la robinetterie viennent de chez Boffi. Les étagères sont en pruche.*
En bas : *Dans le salon, la pièce de résistance : un immense bureau en sycomore réalisé sur mesure par Mahdavi.*

Rechts: *Waschbecken und Armaturen sind von Boffi. Die Schränke sind aus Kiefernholz.*
Unten: *Das Glanzstück im Wohnzimmer ist der von Mahdavi sonderangefertigte riesige Schreibtisch aus Platanenholz.*

Above: An antique banquette stands at the foot of the bed.
Right: Two steel and opalescent-glass doors add an avant-garde touch
to the apartment's corridor.

En haut : Une banquette ancienne devant le lit.
À droite : Deux portes en acier et verre opalescent confèrent un côté
avant-gardiste au couloir de l'appartement.

Oben: Ein antikes Sofa steht vor dem Bett.
Rechts: Zwei Türen aus Stahlrahmen mit mattiertem Glas verleihen
dem Flur eine avantgardistische Note.

Bertrand Burgalat's life is all about music. He has arranged, composed or produced about a hundred albums, created remixes for Depeche Mode and worked with the controversial writer Michel Houellebecq. He also has his own recording label, Tricatel. A grand piano and electric harpsichord stand in the living room of his apartment. The latter looks out onto the picturesque Square des Batignolles – of which he has been particularly fond since he was a child. "It feels more like you're in the provinces than Paris," he states. The flat itself also has musical connections. Its former owner was Edith Piaf's impresario, Loulou Barrier, who bequeathed both the bookshelves and sofas to Burgalat. Since taking it over, he has been keen to maintain its spirit. "I simply repainted the walls and changed the carpet," he says. "I daren't change anything else. I'm too scared to ruin it!"

Bertrand Burgalat

Toute la vie de Bertrand Burgalat tourne autour de la musique. Il a arrangé, composé ou produit une centaine de disques, créé des remix pour Depeche Mode et collaboré avec l'écrivain sulfureux Michel Houellebecq. Il possède également son propre label, Tricatel. Un piano à queue et un clavecin électrique dominent son séjour qui donne sur le pittoresque square des Batignolles, un quartier qu'il aime depuis son enfance. « On a l'impression d'être plus en province qu'à Paris », explique-t-il. Même l'appartement a un rapport avec la musique. Son ancien propriétaire était Loulou Barrier, l'impresario d'Edith Piaf. Il a légué sa bibliothèque et ses canapés à Burgalat, qui s'est efforcé de conserver l'esprit des lieux. « J'ai simplement refait la peinture et la moquette. Structurellement, je n'ose rien changer. J'ai trop peur de le charcuter, cet appartement ! »

Bei Bertrand Burgalat dreht sich alles um Musik. Er hat ungefähr hundert Alben arrangiert, komponiert oder produziert, Remixes für Depeche Mode gemacht oder mit dem umstrittenen Autor Michel Houellebecq zusammengearbeitet. Er besitzt auch ein eigenes Plattenlabel namens Tricatel. Ein Flügel und eine Elektro-Orgel stehen im Wohnzimmer seines Appartements. Von Letzterem schaut man auf den malerischen Square des Batignolles hinaus – ein Platz, den Burgalat schon seit Kindertagen ins Herz geschlossen hat. »Hier kommt man sich eher vor wie in der Provinz und nicht wie in Paris«, sagt er. Auch die Wohnung selbst hat eine musikalische Vergangenheit. Ihr früherer Besitzer war Loulou Barrier, der Impresario von Edith Piaf. Er überließ Burgalat sowohl die Bücherregale als auch die Sofas. Seit der Musiker die Wohnung übernahm, hat er genau darauf geachtet, das ursprüngliche Flair zu erhalten. »Ich habe bloß die Wände gestrichen und einen neuen Teppich verlegt«, sagt er. »Mehr habe ich mich nicht getraut zu tun. Ich habe viel zu viel Angst, das Appartement zu ruinieren!«

Previous pages: In the entrance of the building, the concierge's "loge" still has its traditional frontage.
Above: Among the instruments in the living room are a Baldwin electric harpsichord and a Schimmel grand piano.
Right: Louis XVI-style chairs are grouped around an Eames dining table.

Pages précédentes : Dans l'entrée de l'immeuble, la loge de concierge a conservé sa devanture traditionnelle.
En haut : Parmi les instruments qui trônent dans le séjour, un clavecin électrique Baldwin et un piano de concert Schimmel.
À droite : Des chaises de style Louis XVI autour d'une table d'Eames.

Vorhergehende Seiten: Am Eingang des Gebäudes hat die Concierge-loge immer noch ihre traditionelle Fassade.
Oben: Zu den Instrumenten im Wohnzimmer gehören eine Baldwin-Elektro-Orgel und ein Schimmel-Flügel.
Rechts: Stühle im Louis-XVI-Stil stehen um einen Eames-Esstisch.

Right: The Max Walter Svanberg tapestry is entitled "Le Baiser de la Femme de Rêve" (The Kiss of the Dream Woman).
Below: The former owner, Loulou Barrier, left the two sofas for Burgalat. The one on the right is from Maison Jansen. In the corner, a fake fern has been mounted on a wooden column.
Following pages: Burgalat's record collection is arranged by style of music. When closed, the 1960s record player resembles a die. On the right of the radiator is a silver cigarette box, which once belonged to Italian writer Gabriele D'Annunzio. An old 16mm Bolex camera. The head-shaped object to the right of the piano is a Neumann studio microphone.

À droite : La tapisserie réalisée d'après un carton de Max Walter Svanberg est intitulée « Le Baiser de la Femme de Rêve ».
En bas : L'ancien propriétaire, Loulou Barrier, a laissé les deux canapés à Burgalat. Celui de droite vient de la maison Jansen. Dans le coin, une fausse fougère posée sur une colonne en bois.
Pages suivantes : La collection de disques de Burgalat est classée par styles de musique. Fermé, le tourne-disque des années 1960 forme un dé à jouer. Sur la droite du radiateur, un étui à cigarettes en argent ayant appartenu à l'écrivain italien Gabriele D'Annunzio. Une vieille caméra 16mm Bolex. L'objet en forme de tête à droite du piano est un micro de studio Neumann.

Rechts: Der Wandteppich von Max Walter Svanberg heißt »Le Baiser de la Femme de Rêve« (»Der Kuss der Traumfrau«).
Unten: Der frühere Eigentümer Loulou Barrier überließ Burgalat beide Sofas. Das Rechte ist von Maison Jansen.
Folgende Seiten: Burgalats Plattensammlung ist nach Musikstilen sortiert. Der Plattenspieler aus den 1960er-Jahren sieht geschlossen aus wie ein Würfel. Rechts von der Heizung befindet sich eine silberne Zigarettendose, die einst dem italienischen Schriftsteller Gabriele D'Annunzio gehörte. Eine alte 16mm-Bolex-Kamera. Der Kopf rechts vom Flügel ist ein Neumann-Studio-Mikrofon.

In 2004, architect Sébastien Segers received a call from a client, himself a designer. "I've seen an extraordinary house," he was told. "We've got to find the owner." The house in question is situated near the Parc des Buttes-Chaumont and was built in 1953 by a French architect called Fernand Riehl as his own home and office. It was lying more or less abandoned. "The previous owner," says Segers, "had ripped out almost everything inside." The new owner masterminded the restoration as he wanted to ensure that it would be as sympathetic to the original as possible. Outside the windows and concrete detailing were restored. Inside, the layout was more or less maintained and traditional materials, such as Carrara marble in the bathroom and leather for the upstairs flooring were employed. A touch of modernity was added with the inclusion of rounded architectural forms and numerous design classics pieces. "I can't imagine getting rid of this place," states the owner. "It's unique."

Les Buttes-Chaumont

En 2004, l'architecte Sébastien Segers reçut l'appel d'un client, lui-même designer : « J'ai vu une maison extraordinaire. Il faut trouver le propriétaire ! ». Située près du parc des Buttes-Chaumont, la maison en question, plus ou moins abandonnée, fut construite en 1953 par l'architecte Fernand Riehl pour y vivre et travailler. « Le précédent occupant avait déjà presque tout détruit à l'intérieur » explique Segers. Le nouveau propriétaire a conçu la restauration qu'il voulait la plus respectueuse possible de l'original. Les fenêtres et les détails en béton de la façade ont été restaurés, à l'intérieur le plan au sol a été plus ou moins conservé en utilisant des matériaux traditionnels tels que le marbre de Carrare pour la salle de bains et le cuir pour le sol à l'étage. Des formes architecturales arrondies et des meubles design apportent à l'ensemble une touche de modernité. « Je ne peux imaginer me défaire de cet endroit. Il est unique » déclare le maître des lieux.

Im Jahr 2004 erhielt der Architekt Sébastien Segers einen Anruf von einem seiner Kunden, der selbst Designer ist. »Ich habe ein außergewöhnliches Haus entdeckt«, bekam er zu hören. »Wir müssen den Eigentümer ausfindig machen.« Das fragliche Haus liegt unweit des Parc des Buttes-Chaumont und wurde 1953 von dem französischen Architekten Fernand Riehl als dessen Wohnhaus und Büro gebaut. Inzwischen lag es mehr oder weniger verlassen da. »Der Vorbesitzer«, so Segers, »hatte beinahe alles rausgerissen.« Der neue Besitzer entwarf das Konzept für die Restaurierung, dabei wollte er dem Original so weit wie möglich Rechnung tragen. An der Fassade wurden die Fenster und Betondetails wieder hergestellt. Das Innere wurde größtenteils beibehalten: Es wurden traditionelle Materialien wie Carrara-Marmor im Bad und Leder für den Bodenbelag im Obergeschoss verwendet. Durch die Einbettung runder architektonischer Formen und zahlreicher Designklassiker wurde für einen modernen Touch gesorgt. »Ich kann mir nicht vorstellen, das Haus je wieder aufzugeben«, so der jetzige Eigentümer. »Es ist einzigartig.«

Previous pages: *Both the office desk and chair were designed by Marc Newson. In the dining room, Achille Castiglioni's "Arco" lamp hangs over a table made from African bubinga wood.*
Above: *The custom, sheet-metal doors of the kitchen units were painted a powder blue to match the Aga range.*
Right: *Traditional Carrara marble in the first-floor bathroom.*
Facing page: *A Franco Albini shelving system in the office.*
Following pages: *On the first floor, a foldaway blue lacquered screen can be extended in order to enclose the master bedroom.*

Pages précédentes : *Le bureau et le fauteuil ont été dessinés par Marc Newson. Dans la salle à manger, un lampadaire « Arco » d'Achille Castiglioni éclaire une table en bubinga africain.*
En haut : *Les placards bleu pastel harmonisent avec la cuisinière Aga.*
À droite : *Dans la salle de bains le marbre de Carrare traditionnel.*
Page de droite : *Dans le bureau, une bibliothèque de Franco Albini.*
Pages suivantes : *Au premier étage, le paravent en laque bleu se déploie pour préserver l'intimité de la chambre à coucher.*

Vorhergehende Seiten: *Büroschreibtisch und Stuhl sind Entwürfe von Marc Newson. Im Esszimmer hängt Achille Castiglionis »Arco«-Lampe über einem Tisch aus afrikanischem Bubinga-Holz.*
Oben: *Die Blechtüren der speziell angefertigten Küche wurden in einem pudrigen Blauton gestrichen, damit sie zum Herd von Aga passen.*
Rechts: *Carrara-Marmor im Bad.*
Gegenüberliegende Seite: *Das Regalsystem von Franco Albini im Büro.*
Folgende Seiten: *Im ersten Stock lässt sich ein blau lackierter Wandschirm ausklappen, um das Schlafzimmer abzugrenzen.*

When the owners of this duplex in the 16th arrondissement first saw it, they immediately realised it would be the perfect setting for an art collection. It's easy to see why. The double-height sitting room has both a huge window and a skylight, reminiscent of a painter's studio. Working with art consultant Philippe Ségalot, they particularly like making acquisitions in the United States because of the buzz they feel there. They collect works by Warhol and Murakami, photos by Cindy Sherman and Hiroshi Sugimoto, and have a passion for the drawings of Raymond Pettibon. They claim that once you start collecting them, you can't stop. And their favourite work? A self-portrait of Jean-Michel Basquiat, whose skeleton-like form seems to presage the artist's untimely death.

Collectionneurs d'Art

Dès le premier coup d'œil, les propriétaires de ce duplex du 16ᵉ arrondissement ont su qu'il était idéal pour abriter leur collection d'art. En effet, avec son immense fenêtre, sa verrière et sa double hauteur sous plafond, le séjour rappelle un atelier d'artiste. Avec l'aide du consultant Philippe Ségalot, ils achètent surtout aux États-Unis, où le monde de l'art leur semble plus palpitant. Ils collectionnent des œuvres de Warhol, de Murakami, de Cindy Sherman et ont une passion pour les dessins de Raymond Pettibon. Selon eux, une fois qu'on commence à les collectionner, on ne peut plus s'arrêter. Leur œuvre préférée ? Un autoportrait de Jean-Michel Basquiat, dont la silhouette squelettique semble présager la mort prématurée de l'artiste.

Als die Eigentümer dieser Duplexwohnung im 16. Arrondissement die Wohnung zum ersten Mal besichtigten, sahen sie gleich, dass sie den perfekten Rahmen für eine Kunstsammlung bietet. Das ist mehr als offensichtlich: Der hohe Wohnraum mit Galerie hat sowohl ein riesiges Fenster als auch ein Oberlicht, womit er an das Atelier eines Malers erinnert. Die Besitzer arbeiten viel mit dem Kunstberater Philippe Ségalot zusammen und kaufen besonders gern Kunst in den Vereinigten Staaten, weil dort eine besondere Energie herrscht. Sie sammeln Arbeiten von Warhol und Murakami, Fotos von Cindy Sherman und Hiroshi Sugimoto und begeistern sich für die Zeichnungen von Raymond Pettibon. Sie sagen, hätte man erst einmal mit dem Sammeln begonnen, könne man nicht mehr aufhören. Und ihre Lieblingsarbeit? Ein Selbstporträt von Jean-Michel Basquiat, dessen skelettartige Form den viel zu frühen Tod des Künstlers vorwegzunehmen scheint.

Previous pages: A Takashi Murakami sculpture in the dining room entitled "Tatsuya."
Above: An India Mahdavi bench, two Marc Newson standing lights and a carpet from Diurne in Paris can be seen in the entrance hall.
Right: Another Murakami sculpture, called "The Mushroom", from the Galerie Emmanuel Perrotin.

Pages précédentes : Dans la salle à manger, une statue de Takashi Murakami intitulée « Tatsuya ».
En haut : Dans l'entrée, un banc d'India Mahdavi, deux luminaires de Marc Newson et un tapis de la galerie parisienne Diurne.
À droite : Une autre sculpture de Murakami, « The Mushroom », de la Galerie Emmanuel Perrotin.

Vorhergehende Seiten: Eines der Fotos von Hiroshi Sugimoto zeigt die Wachsfigur von Elizabeth I. in Madame Tussaud's in London. Eine Skulptur von Takashi Murakami mit dem Titel »Tatsuya« im Esszimmer.
Oben: Eine Bank von India Mahdavi, zwei Stehlampen von Marc Newson und ein Teppich von Diurne, Paris, schmücken den Flur.
Rechts: Eine weitere Skulptur von Murakami mit dem Titel »The Mushroom«, von der Galerie Emmanuel Perrotin.

Right: *The huge painting called "The Porter" is by Jean-Michel Basquiat.*
Below: *An interesting mix of styles in the living room: Jean Royère armchairs and ottoman, Christian Liaigre sofas and standing lights on the right by the Bouroullec brothers and Alberto Giacometti.*

À droite : *L'immense toile intitulée « The Porter » est de Jean-Michel Basquiat.*
En bas : *Dans le séjour, un intéressant mélange de styles : un pouf et des fauteuils de Jean Royère, des canapés Christian Liaigre et, sur la droite, des lampadaires des frères Bouroullec et d'Alberto Giacometti.*

Rechts: *Das große Gemälde mit dem Titel »The Porter« stammt von Jean-Michel Basquiat.*
Unten: *Eine interessante Mischung im Wohnzimmer: zwei Sessel und eine Ottomane von Jean Royère, Sofas von Christian Liaigre, rechts davon eine Stehlampe von den Brüdern Bouroullec und dahinter eine von Alberto Giacometti.*

Decorators Michael Coorengel and Jean-Pierre Calvagrac are modern-day dandies with a penchant for extravagance. Take their 250-square-metre apartment, located in an 1836 town mansion in the 10th arrondissement, built by Baron Louis, a protégé of the French states-man Talleyrand. Each room is more sumptuous than the next. One has been painted silver. Another has jet-black walls and golden mouldings. Throughout, the furnishings are a mix of their differing styles. Coorengel likes all things baroque, Calvagrac prefers modern design. The result is really quite thrilling. An early 19th-century méridienne has been reupholstered in a shocking green silk and a Mies van der Rohe "Barcelona" chair juxtaposed with a bed in which Napoleon is said to have slept! "Our goal," they claim, "is to find a happy medium between our two creative worlds."

Michael Coorengel & Jean-Pierre Calvagrac

Les décorateurs Michael Coorengel et Jean-Pierre Calvagrac sont deux dandys modernes avec un faible pour l'extravagance. Leur appartement de 250 mètres carrés a été construit en 1836 par le baron Louis, un protégé de Talleyrand. Chaque pièce surpasse la précédente en somptuosité. Une est peinte en argent, une autre en noir comme du jais avec des moulures dorées. Le mobilier éclectique reflète leurs goûts différents. Coorengel aime le baroque, Calvagrac préfère le design moderne. Le résultat est fascinant. Une méridienne du début du XIXe siècle a été retapissée en soie vert shocking et un fauteuil « Barcelona » de Mies van der Rohe côtoie un lit où Napoléon aurait dormi ! « Notre objectif est de trouver un équilibre harmonieux entre deux univers créatifs », déclarent-ils.

Die Innenausstatter Michael Coorengel und Jean-Pierre Calvagrac sind moderne Dandys mit einem Hang zur Extravaganz. Das zeigt auch ihre 250 Quadratmeter große Wohnung in einer Stadtvilla von 1836, die sich im 10. Arrondissement befindet und von einem Schützling des französischen Staatsmannes Talleyrand namens Baron Louis erbaut wurde. Die Zimmer scheinen sich in ihrer Opulenz gegenseitig übertrumpfen zu wollen. Eines wurde ganz in Silber gestrichen, ein anderes verfügt über pechschwarze Wände mit vergoldeten Stuckverzierungen. Die Möbel sind eine Mischung aus verschiedenen Stilen. Coorengel mag alles, was barock ist, Calvagrac bevorzugt modernes Design. Das Ergebnis ist ziemlich aufregend. Eine Chaiselongue aus dem frühen 19. Jahrhundert wurde mit grellgrüner Seide neu bezogen und Mies van der Rohes »Barcelona«-Sessel mit einem Bett kombiniert, in dem angeblich Napoleon geschlafen haben soll! »Unser Ziel«, so die beiden, »besteht darin, den goldenen Mittelweg zwischen unseren kreativen Welten zu finden.«

Previous pages: In the "Silver Room", two Marcel Breuer chairs sit either side of a 1960s dining table. The Louis XVI sofa is thought to have been created for the Petit Trianon at Versailles.
Above: A Mies van der Rohe "Barcelona" chair, a George Nakashima coffee table, and a bed in which Napoleon is said to have slept.
Right: A bust of Demosthenes and obelisks adorn the master bathroom.
Facing page: A buffet stocked with sterling silver and nautilus shells.
Following pages: A shocking green Empire banquette stands on a Verner Panton rug in the opulent "Gold Room".

Pages précédentes : Dans le « salon argenté », deux fauteuils de Marcel Breuer de chaque côté d'une table des années 1960. Le canapé Louis XVI aurait été créé pour le Petit Trianon à Versailles.
En haut : Un fauteuil « Barcelona » de Mies van der Rohe, une table basse de George Nakashima et un lit dans lequel Napoléon aurait dormi.
À droite : Un buste de Démosthène et des obélisques des années 1940 dans la salle de bains des maîtres de maison.
Page de droite : Un buffet rempli d'argenterie et de nautiles.
Pages suivantes : Une banquette Empire vert shocking sur un tapis de Verner Panton dans l'opulent « salon doré ».

Vorhergehende Seiten: Im »Silbernen Zimmer« rahmen zwei Marcel-Breuer-Stühle einen Esstisch aus den 1960er-Jahren ein. Das Louis-XVI-Sofa soll für das Petit Trianon in Versailles gefertigt worden sein.
Oben: Ein Bett, in dem Napoleon geschlafen haben soll.
Rechts: Eine Büste des Demosthenes und Obelisken aus den 1940er-Jahren schmücken das Bad.
Gegenüberliegende Seite: Ein Küchenbüfett aus dem 16. Jahrhundert, das mit Sterlingsilber und mit Nautilusmuscheln bestückt ist.
Folgende Seiten: Eine grellgrün bezogene Empire-Liege auf einem Teppich von Verner Panton im opulenten »Goldenen Zimmer«.

New Paris Interiors Michael Coorengel & Jean-Pierre Calvagrac

For 12 years, Alexandre de Betak's main base has been New York. It's from there that he masterminds special events and fashion shows for the likes of Christian Dior and Victoria's Secret. When he and his model fiancée Audrey Marnay decided to buy a pied-à-terre in Paris, they opted for the type of place that the citizens of their adopted America generally favour. "I had a fantasy of a really traditional flat in a touristy area," he admits. Situated near Trocadéro, the largely black-and-white apartment is filled with intriguing kinetic objects and "weird lights", one of which originally belonged to a Long Island gay club. There are also a whole host of robots, which Betak has brought back from Japan, and a number of his own furniture creations. Among them are the daybed in the living room and the Plexiglas bookshelves in his office.

Alexandre de Betak

Alexandre de Betak est basé à New York depuis douze ans. C'est de là-bas qu'il organise des événements et des défilés pour des clients tels que Christian Dior ou Victoria's Secret. Quand sa fiancée, le mannequin Audrey Marnay, et lui ont décidé d'acheter un pied-à-terre à Paris, ils ont opté pour le genre d'endroit que privilégient habituellement les citoyens de leur pays d'adoption. « J'ai eu envie d'un appartement très classique dans un endroit pour touristes », avoue-t-il. Situé près du Trocadéro, l'appartement où domine le noir et blanc est rempli de curieux objets cinétiques et de « lumières bizarroïdes », dont l'une provient d'un club gay de Long Island. On y trouve aussi une foule de robots rapportés du Japon et de meubles créés par Betak. Parmi eux, le lit de repos du séjour et les étagères en plexiglas de son bureau.

Seit zwölf Jahren lebt der Franzose Alexandre de Betak eigentlich überwiegend in New York. Von dort aus organisiert er Spezialevents und Modeschauen zum Beispiel für Christian Dior und Victoria's Secret. Als er und seine Freundin, das Model Audrey Marnay, beschlossen, sich ein Pied-à-terre in Paris zu kaufen, suchten sie sich einen Ort aus, wie er normalerweise von Amerikanern bevorzugt wird. »Ich träumte von einer ganz traditionellen Wohnung in einem Touristen- viertel«, gibt er zu. Das unweit der Place du Trocadéro gelegene Appartement ist überwiegend in Schwarz-Weiß gehalten und zum Teil mit eigenen Möbelentwürfen eingerichtet, wie die Liege im Wohn- und die Plexiglasregale im Arbeitszimmer. Und es steckt voller faszinierender kinetischer Objekte und »verrückter« Lampen, so stammt eine davon ursprünglich aus einem Schwulenclub auf Long Island. Es gibt auch ganze Armeen von Robotern, die Betak meist aus Japan mitgebracht hat.

Previous pages: In the living room, a 1960s prototype of a chair by Jørgen Kastholm stands beneath a light sculpture by Gianfranco Fini. The 1970s chrome lamp was bought on New York's Lower East Side.
Above: Betak created the neon installation entitled "Gisèle's Bra and Hair" for a Victoria's Secret event. His leather and Plexiglas daybed is produced by Domeau & Pérès.
Right: Betak designed both the table and benches in the kitchen. As elsewhere, there are numerous light sculptures, including a glass cube on the floor, by André Cazenave.

Pages précédentes : Dans le séjour, un prototype d'une chaise de Jørgen Kastholm sous une sculpture lumineuse de Gianfranco Fini. La lampe chromée des années 1970 a été achetée dans le Lower East Side à New York.
En haut : Betak a créé l'installation en néon intitulée « Gisèle's Bra and Hair » pour un événement de Victoria's Secret. Son lit de repos en cuir et plexiglas est édité par Domeau & Pérès.
À droite : Betak a dessiné la table et les bancs de la cuisine. Comme toutes les pièces, celle-ci accueille de nombreuses sculptures lumineuses dont un cube en verre d'André Cazenave.

Vorhergehende Seiten: Im Wohnzimmer steht der Prototyp eines Stuhls von Jørgen Kastholm unter einer Lichtskulptur von Gianfranco Fini, die Betak in Berlin entdeckte. Die Chromlampe aus den 1970er-Jahren wurde in der New Yorker Lower East Side erworben.
Oben: Betak selbst schuf die Neon-Installation mit dem Titel »Gisèle's Bra and Hair« für ein Event von Victoria's Secret. Seine Liege aus Leder und Plexiglas wird von Domeau & Pérès produziert.
Rechts: Betak entwarf den Tisch und auch die Bänke in der Küche. Wie überall gibt es hier zahlreiche Leuchtskulpturen wie den Glaswürfel auf dem Boden von André Cazenave.

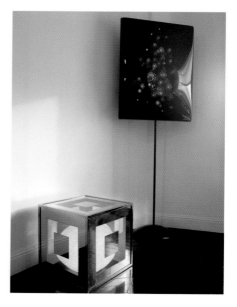

Right: In the kitchen, the light sculpture is by Giacomo Benevelli. The collection of robots comes mainly from Japan.
Below: In the sitting room, a pair of Catherine Memmi sofas flanks coffee tables of Betak's own design. The two resin casts of turtle shells date from the 1970s. Hanging in the far left corner is a 1960s kinetic sculpture by Gianni Colombo.
Following pages: The Plexiglas bookshelves in the office were designed by Betak. On a table in the same room are silvered glass balls, which Betak had made for a light installation. The photo of Betak was taken by Karl Lagerfeld and the portrait of a pregnant Marnay by Jean-Baptiste Mondino.

À droite : Dans la cuisine une sculpture lumineuse de Giacomo Benevelli. La collection de robots vient principalement du Japon.
En bas : Dans le séjour, une paire de canapés Catherine Memmi flanquent des tables basses dessinées par Betak. Les deux carapaces de tortue en résine datent des années 1970. Suspendue dans l'angle, une sculpture cinétique de Gianni Colombo des années 1960.
Pages suivantes : Betak a dessiné les étagères en plexiglas de son bureau. Sur la table, des boules en verre argenté que Betak a fait faire pour une installation lumineuse. La photo de Betak est de Karl Lagerfeld et celle de Marnay enceinte est de Jean-Baptiste Mondino.

Rechts: Die Lichtskulptur in der Küche ist von Giacomo Benevelli. Die Robotersammlung kommt überwiegend aus Japan.
Unten: Im Wohnzimmer wurden zwei Sofas von Catherine Memmi um Couchtische gruppiert, die Betak selbst entworfen hat. Die beiden Gießharzgüsse von Schildkrötenpanzern sind aus den 1970er-Jahren.
Folgende Seiten: Die Plexiglasregale im Arbeitszimmer wurden von Betak entworfen. Auf einem Tisch im selben Zimmer befinden sich versilberte Glaskugeln, die Betak für eine Lichtinstallation anfertigen ließ. Das Foto von Betak wurde von Karl Lagerfeld aufgenommen, und das Porträt der schwangeren Marnay ist von Jean-Baptiste Mondino.

Facing page: The couple has two sons, Aidyn Anakyn and Amaël.
The cartoon character in Aidyn Anakyn's bedroom was drawn by the
graffiti artist André. The mobile on the ceiling represents planets.
Above: In one corner of the living room is an old architect's table
and an industrial stool. A white "Robosapiens" toy stands on a 1970s
Italian light sculpture.
Right: Betak designed the master bed from stained, sanded oak. The
multi-coloured light on the floor is a 1980s disco ball.

Page de gauche : La chambre de l'un des deux fils du couple, Aidyn
Anakyn et Amaël. Le personnage de dessin animé a été peint par
l'artiste de graffiti André. Le mobile représente les planètes.
En haut : Dans un coin du séjour, un vieux bureau d'architecte et un
tabouret industriel. Un jouet « Robosapiens » blanc sur une sculpture
lumineuse italienne des années 1970.
À droite : Dans la chambre des maîtres, Betak a créé un lit en chêne
sablé et teinté. Au sol, une boule disco multicolore des années 1980.

Gegenüberliegende Seite: Das Paar hat zwei Söhne, Aidyn Anakyn
und Amaël. Die Comicfigur in Aidyn Anakyns Zimmer zeichnete der
Graffiti-Künstler André. Das Mobile an der Decke zeigt eine Planeten-
konstellation.
Oben: In einer Ecke des Wohnzimmers stehen ein alter Zeichentisch
und ein Industriestuhl. Ein weißer »Robosapiens« steht auf einer
italienischen Lichtskulptur aus den 1970er-Jahren.
Rechts: Betak entwarf das Bett aus gebeizter, geschliffener Eiche. Das
bunte Licht auf dem Boden ist eine Discolampe aus den 1980er-Jahren.

Antique dealer Franck Delmarcelle runs a boutique called Et Caetera in the Marais district, which is frequented by the likes of John Galliano and Christian Lacroix. He describes his style as "poor chic." "By that," he explains, "I mean objects that don't necessarily have an intrinsic value, but that have a soul." His 50-square-metre flat is full of them. The paint on the dining chairs is slightly worn. An 18th-century plaster statue looks like it has been left out in the rain and a Louis XVI sofa in the bedroom still has its original Aubusson tapestry. Throughout, there are numerous examples of taxidermy – a horse's head, a lizard and several stuffed birds. There is also a cabinet de curiosités and religious paraphernalia – altar decorations, a limestone cross and even a statue of the Virgin Mary.

Franck Delmarcelle

Et Caetera, la boutique de l'antiquaire Franck Delmarcelle dans le Marais, attire des sommités tels que John Galliano et Christian Lacroix. Il définit lui-même son style « chic pauvre ». « J'entends par là des objets qui n'ont pas forcément une valeur intrinsèque mais qui ont une âme. » Son appartement de 50 mètres carrés n'en manque pas. Les chaises de sa salle à manger sont légèrement défraîchies. Une statue en plâtre du XVIIIᵉ siècle semble avoir été oubliée sous la pluie et le sofa Louis XVI dans la chambre possède encore sa tapisserie d'Aubusson d'origine. Il a un faible pour la taxidermie : on croise chez lui une tête de cheval, un lézard et plusieurs oiseaux empaillés. On trouve également un cabinet de curiosités et des objets religieux : des décors d'autels, une croix en calcaire et même une statue de la Vierge Marie.

Dem Antiquitätenhändler Franck Delmarcelle gehört ein Laden namens Et Caetera im Marais, zu dessen Kunden John Galliano und Christian Lacroix zählen. Er beschreibt seinen Stil als »poor chic«: »Damit meine ich Einrichtungsgegenstände, die an und für sich nicht wertvoll sind, aber eine Seele haben«, erklärt er. Seine 50 Quadratmeter große Wohnung ist voll davon. Der Lack der Esszimmerstühle ist bereits etwas abgeblättert. Eine Gipsstatue aus dem 18. Jahrhundert sieht aus, als hätte sie jemand im Regen vergessen, und das Louis-XVI-Sofa im Schlafzimmer besitzt immer noch seinen originalen Aubusson-Bezug. Überall finden sich präparierte Tiere – ein Pferdekopf, eine Echse und diverse ausgestopfte Vögel. Es gibt auch ein Kuriositäten-kabinett sowie zahlreiche religiöse Devotionalien – Altardekorationen, ein Kreuz aus Kalkstein und auch eine Statue der Jungfrau Maria.

Previous pages: The elm dining table probably comes from a convent. The chairs have been reupholstered in an 18th-century linen.
Facing page: Altar decorations in the form of brass lilies and an allegorical painting sit atop a Louis XV-style console table. The limestone cross comes from a chapel in Picardy.
Above: Two 19th-century armchairs stand either side of a dresser.
Right: A painting of a pot of geraniums hangs above the kitchen sink.

Pages précédentes : La table de salle à manger en orme provient d'un couvent. Les chaises ont été retapissées avec du lin du XVIIIᵉ siècle.
Page de gauche : Des ornements d'autel en laiton en forme de lis et une allégorie sur une console de style Louis XV. La croix en calcaire vient d'une chapelle de Picardie.
En haut : Deux fauteuils du XIXᵉ siècle encadrent un vaisselier.
À droite : Une peinture représentant un pot de géraniums au-dessus de l'évier de la cuisine.

Vorhergehende Seiten: Der Esstisch aus Ulmenholz stammt wahrscheinlich aus einem Nonnenkloster. Die Stühle aus dem 19. Jahrhundert wurden mit Leinen aus dem 18. Jahrhundert bezogen.
Gegenüberliegende Seite: Altardekorationen sowie ein allegorisches Gemälde schmücken einen Konsoltisch im Louis-XV-Stil. Das Kalksteinkreuz stammt aus einer Kapelle in der Picardie.
Oben: Zwei Sessel aus dem 19. Jahrhundert rahmen eine Anrichte aus dem 18. Jahrhundert ein.
Rechts: Ein Gemälde mit Geranien hängt über der Küchenspüle.

Facing page: Delmarcelle created a washed linen slip cover for the Louis XVIII sofa. To its left is an 18th-century garden sculpture and to its right a Virgin made from plaster, dating from c. 1900.

Page de droite : Delmarcelle a créé la housse en lin délavé du canapé Louis XVIII. Il est flanqué, à gauche, d'une statue de jardin du XVIIIᵉ siècle et, à droite, d'une Vierge en plâtre datant de 1900 environ.

Gegenüberliegende Seite: Für das Louis-XVIII-Sofa fertigte Delmarcelle einen verwaschenen Leinenüberzug an. Links steht eine Gartenskulptur aus dem 18. Jahrhundert und rechts eine Marienstatue aus Gips, die etwa um 1900 geschaffen wurde.

Above: The Louis XVI sofa in the bedroom still has its original Aubusson tapestry upholstery. The corner chest dates from the Empire period.
Right: The bedroom mirror was created using the frame of a bull's-eye window. On the Directoire bedside table is the "Bourgie" lamp, designed by Ferruccio Laviani for Kartell.

En haut : Le sofa Louis XVI dans la chambre possède encore sa tapisserie d'Aubusson d'origine. L'encoignure date de la période Empire.
À droite : Le miroir dans la chambre a été créé en recyclant le cadre d'un œil-de-bœuf. Sur la table de nuit Directoire, une lampe « Bourgie », dessinée par Ferruccio Laviani pour Kartell.

Oben: Das Louis-XVI-Sofa im Schlafzimmer besitzt immer noch seinen originalen Aubusson-Bezug. Die Eckkommode stammt aus der Empire-Zeit.
Rechts: Der Schlafzimmerspiegel entstand, indem der Rahmen eines Butzenfensters verwendet wurde. Auf dem Directoire-Nachttisch steht die »Bourgie«-Lampe, ein Entwurf von Ferruccio Laviani für Kartell.

Decorator Jean-Louis Deniot is a world traveller. He has projects in places like Delhi and Colombia, and five residences between France and the United States. Among them is a 45-square-metre pied-à-terre in the Saint-Germain-des-Prés district, which perfectly reflects his philosophy about small spaces – that you should bestow them with great refinement. "That way," he says, "you compensate for the lack of space." He covered the walls with fake parchment and had the doors stylishly painted to resemble rosewood. He also filled the two main rooms with a plethora of objects. "If you do something too minimalist, small apartments immediately look like shoeboxes," he opines. Most cleverly, he integrated a maximum of storage throughout. In the bedroom, he devised two walk-in dressing rooms and created drawers in the base of the bed. He also hid a small office space and a tiny kitchen behind doors in the living room.

Jean-Louis Deniot

Jean-Louis Deniot est un décorateur globe-trotter, sillonnant la planète de New Delhi à la Colombie. Parmi ses cinq résidences réparties entre la France et les États-Unis, son pied-à-terre de 45 mètres carrés à Saint-Germain-des-Prés reflète parfaitement sa philosophie des petits espaces : un raffinement extrême permet de compenser le manque de place. Les murs sont tapissés de faux parchemin et les portes peintes en trompe-l'œil de bois de rose. Les deux pièces principales sont remplies d'objets. « Trop minimalistes, les petits appartements ressemblent à des boîtes à chaussures », observe-t-il. Partout, il a imaginé des espaces de rangement astucieux : dans la chambre, il a conçu deux dressings et des tiroirs encastrés dans le sommier du lit ; dans le salon, des portes cachent un petit bureau et une kitchenette.

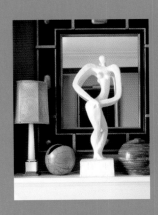

Der Innenausstatter Jean-Louis Deniot ist ein Mann von Welt. Er hat Projekte in Delhi und Kolumbien sowie fünf Wohnsitze zwischen Frankreich und den USA. Dazu gehört auch ein 45 Quadratmeter großes Pied-à-terre im Viertel Saint-Germain-des-Prés, das seine Philosophie hinsichtlich kleiner Räume perfekt illustriert – nämlich, dass man sie mit großer Raffinesse einrichten sollte. »Auf diese Weise kann man den Platzmangel hervorragend kompensieren.« Er bespannte die Wände mit falschem Pergament und ließ die Türen so bemalen, dass sie an Rosenholz erinnern. Außerdem dekorierte er die beiden Haupträume mit einer Fülle von Objekten, denn »wenn man zu minimalistisch vorgeht, sehen kleine Appartements schnell aus wie Schuhschachteln.« Höchst geschickt hat er überall ein Maximum an Stauraum geschaffen. Im Flur beherbergt ein Schrank die Waschmaschine. Im Schlafzimmer gestaltete er zwei begehbare Kleiderschränke und integrierte Schubladen in den Bettsockel. Hinter Türen im Wohnzimmer versteckte er sogar ein kleines Büro und eine winzige Küche.

Previous pages: A minuscule kitchen is tucked behind a pair of double doors in the sitting room. The Modénature armchair has been reupholstered in chocolate-coloured pony skin.
Right: A 1940s coffee table and a 1920s plaster column stand on a bold, Madeleine Castaing-designed rug.
Below: Both the green armchairs and the elegant stone fireplace were designed by Deniot.

Pages précédentes : Dans le salon, les doubles portes cachent une minuscule kitchenette. Le fauteuil Modénature a été retapissé en poulain couleur chocolat.
À droite : Une table basse des années 1940 et un socle en plâtre des années 1920 sur un tapis aux couleurs vives dessiné par Madeleine Castaing.
En bas : Deniot a dessiné les fauteuils verts et l'élégante cheminée en pierre.

Vorhergehende Seiten: Hinter einer Doppeltür im Wohnzimmer versteckt sich eine Mini-Küche. Der Modénature-Sessel wurde mit schokoladenfarbenem Ponyfell neu bezogen.
Rechts: Ein Couchtisch aus den 1940er- und eine Gipssäule aus den 1920er-Jahren stehen auf einem gestreiften Teppich, nach einem Entwurf von Madeleine Castaing.
Unten: Sowohl die grünen Sessel als auch der elegante Kamin sind Entwürfe von Deniot.

Above: An early 20th-century copy of a Titian portrait hangs above a Louis XVI sofa. In the background, a 1930s plaster bas-relief can be seen on one wall of the bedroom.
Right: The wall behind the bed is covered with a striped silk from Dominique Kieffer. The 1940s clock was bought at a Paris flea market.

En haut : Une copie d'un portrait du Titien datant du début du XXᵉ siècle au-dessus d'un canapé Louis XVI. Dans le fond, on aperçoit un bas-relief en plâtre des années 1930 sur le mur de la chambre.
À droite : Le mur derrière le lit est tapissé d'une soie rayée de Dominique Kieffer. L'horloge des années 1940 a été chinée au marché aux puces de Paris.

Oben: Die Kopie eines Tizianporträts aus dem frühen 20. Jahrhundert hängt über einem Louis-XVI-Sofa. Im Hintergrund sieht man ein aus den 1930er-Jahren stammendes Gipsrelief an einer der Schlafzimmerwände.
Rechts: Eine gestreifte Seidentapete von Dominique Kieffer schmückt die Wand hinter dem Bett. Die Uhr aus den 1940er-Jahren stammt von einem Pariser Flohmarkt.

Simon de Pury's Parisian pied-à-terre is housed in an 18th-century town mansion in the Marais, built by Claude-Nicolas Ledoux. Author Madame de Staël was born here in 1766. More recently, de Pury's duplex belonged to German artist Anselm Kiefer. De Pury is chairman of the auction house Phillips de Pury & Company and, today, the apartment doubles as offices for the firm's three Parisian employees. The décor is distinctly purist. Objects may be few and far between, but each has an interesting provenance. There are several pieces by Ron Arad, a desk by Martin Szekely, and chairs and a sofa by the Campana brothers. There is also an immense dining table and chairs specially commissioned from Franz West. The former proved so huge that a special crane had to be hired to lift it into the building!

Simon de Pury

Le pied-à-terre de Simon de Pury est situé dans un hôtel particulier du Marais, bâti au XVIIIᵉ siècle par Claude-Nicolas Ledoux. Madame de Staël y est née en 1766. Plus récemment, ce duplex appartenait à l'artiste allemand Anselm Kiefer. Président de la maison de ventes Phillips de Pury & Company, Pury accueille également chez lui les bureaux des trois employés de sa branche parisienne. Le décor est puriste. Les objets sont rares mais chacun a son histoire. Il y a plusieurs pièces de Ron Arad, un bureau de Martin Szekely, des fauteuils et un canapé des frères Campana. La table immense et les chaises qui l'entourent ont été commandées spécialement à l'artiste Franz West. Il a fallu louer une grue pour les hisser dans l'appartement !

Simon de Purys Pariser Pied-à-terre befindet sich im Marais, in einer Stadtvilla aus dem 18. Jahrhundert, die von Claude-Nicolas Ledoux erbaut wurde. Die Schriftstellerin Madame de Staël kam hier 1766 zur Welt, zuletzt gehörte das Duplex dem deutschen Künstler Anselm Kiefer. De Pury ist Präsident des Auktionshauses Phillips de Pury & Company, seine Wohnung dient gleichzeitig als Büro für die drei Pariser Angestellten der Firma. Die Einrichtung ist bewusst reduziert und puristisch. Es gibt nur wenige, locker verteilte Einrichtungsgegenstände, aber ein jeder hat eine interessante Herkunft. Da sind verschiedene Möbel von Ron Arad, ein Tisch von Martin Szekely sowie Stühle und ein Sofa der Campana-Brüder. Der riesige Esstisch ist eine Sonderanfertigung des Künstlers Franz West, von dem auch die Stühle sind. Dieser Tisch musste mit einem Spezialkran in das Gebäude gehievt werden!

Following pages: A series of Mario Testino photos hangs temporarily above de Pury's bed on the upper floor of the duplex. To the left is a 16th-century stone skull and a wooden sculpture of the Madonna and Child. To the right, Axel Salto's "Sprouting Vase" and a ceramic lamp base designed by Georges Jouve.

Pages suivantes : Une série de photos de Mario Testino est provisoirement accrochée au-dessus du lit à l'étage supérieur du duplex. À gauche, un crâne en pierre du XVIᵉ siècle et une sculpture en bois d'une Vierge à l'Enfant. À droite, le « Sprouting Vase » d'Axel Salto et un pied de lampe en céramique dessiné par Georges Jouve.

Folgende Seiten: Eine Fotoserie von Mario Testino hängt vorübergehend über de Purys Bett im oberen Geschoss des Duplex. Links davon befinden sich ein steinerner Totenkopf aus dem 16. Jahrhundert und eine Holzskulptur der Jungfrau Maria mit Kind. Rechts sind Axel Saltos »Sprouting«-Vase und ein Keramiklampenfuß von Georges Jouve zu sehen.

Previous pages: In de Pury's bedroom, the "A.K." desk by Martin Szekely, the "Little Heavy Chair" by Ron Arad and the steel-wire "Corallo" armchair by the Campana brothers.
Facing page: The dining table and chairs were specially commissioned from Franz West. The table top was made from part of the floor of the Austrian artist's studio.
Above and right: The minimalistic kitchen and bathroom reflect de Pury's preference for pared-down spaces.

Pages précédentes : Dans la chambre de Pury, le bureau « A.K. » de Martin Szekely, la « Little Heavy Chair » de Ron Arad et le fauteuil en fil d'acier « Corallo » des frères Campana.
Page de gauche : La table et les chaises de salle à manger ont été commandées spécialement à Franz West. Le plateau de table a été réalisé avec une partie du sol de l'atelier de l'artiste autrichien.
En haut et à droite : La cuisine et la salle de bains minimalistes reflètent le goût de Pury pour les espaces épurés.

Vorhergehende Seiten: In de Purys Schlafzimmer stehen der »A.K.«-Schreibtisch von Martin Szekely, der »Little Heavy Chair« von Ron Arad sowie der Stahldrahtsessel »Corallo« von den Campana-Brüdern.
Gegenüberliegende Seite: Der Esstisch und die Stühle sind eine Spezialanfertigung von Franz West. Die Tischplatte besteht aus einem Teil des Atelierbodens des österreichischen Künstlers.
Oben und rechts: Die minimalistische Küche sowie das Bad spiegeln de Purys Vorliebe für puristische Räume wider.

The Comte and Comtesse Hubert d'Ornano have lived in the same flat for the past 35 years. Originally decorated by the legendary Henri Samuel, it stretches over two floors of an immensely grand building on the Left Bank. Best known as the founders of the skincare and perfume firm Sisley, the couple have also created a style of decoration very much their own. "It's all about mixing things without inhibition," asserts the Comtesse. There are clusters of tables and armchairs, opulent fabrics and rugs, family photos stapled to walls and screens, and numerous works of art. Among them, a portrait of one of the Comtesse's ancestors – Barbara, Queen of Poland – and quirky sculptures of snails and sheep by Jean-François Fourtou. As one commentator judiciously remarked: "There is a grandeur and richness and yet not an ounce of pretence."

Comte & Comtesse Hubert d'Ornano

Le comte et la comtesse Hubert d'Ornano habitent le même appartement depuis 35 ans. Initialement décoré par le légendaire Henri Samuel, il occupe deux étages d'un somptueux immeuble de la rive gauche. Connu pour avoir fondé la maison de cosmétiques et de parfums Sisley, le couple a également créé son propre style de décoration. « On mélange les genres sans inhibition », déclare la comtesse. Des groupes de tables et de fauteuils cohabitent avec de riches étoffes et tapis, des paravents et d'innombrables œuvres d'art. Parmi elles, un portrait d'une ancêtre de la comtesse, Barbara, reine de Pologne, et d'étranges sculptures d'escargots et de moutons de Jean-François Fourtou. Un commentateur a observé judicieusement : « Il y a de la grandeur et de la richesse sans une once de prétention ».

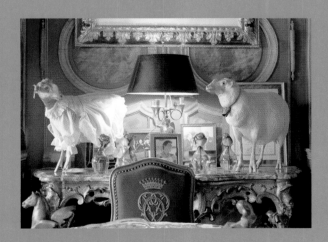

Comte und Comtesse Hubert d'Ornano haben die letzten 35 Jahre immer in derselben Wohnung gelebt. Das ursprünglich vom legendären Henri Samuel eingerichtete Appartement erstreckt sich über zwei Geschosse eines großzügigen, hochherrschaftlichen Gebäudes am linken Seine-Ufer. Das Paar, das vor allem als Gründer der Kosmetik- und Parfümfirma Sisley bekannt wurde, hat einen sehr eigenen Einrichtungsstil kreiert. »Das Geheimnis besteht darin, Dinge ungehemmt miteinander zu kombinieren«, erklärt die Comtesse. Es gibt zahlreiche Gruppen von Tischen und Sesseln, kostbare Stoffe und opulente Teppiche, an Wände und Vertäfelungen gelehnte und gehängte Familienfotos und Kunstwerke. Dazu zählen auch das Porträt der polnischen Königin Barbara, eine Vorfahrin der Comtesse, dazu schräge Skulpturen von Schnecken und Schafen von Jean-François Fourtou. Wie ein Besucher so treffend bemerkte: »Hier findet man Pracht und Reichtum, aber kein bisschen Protz.«

Previous pages: *The green colour was inspired by panelling from Versailles. The crocodile chairs are by Claude Lalanne and the bird sculpture by César.* **Facing page:** *A Louis XIV clock hangs above a Napoleon III sofa in the dining room. The walls are covered in a Bracquenié fabric.* **Above:** *Bronislaw Krzysztof created the table, which depicts the fall of Icarus.*

Pages précédentes : *Le vert des murs a été inspiré par des boiseries du château de Versailles. Les chaises crocodile sont de Claude Lalanne et la sculpture d'oiseau de César.* **Page de gauche :** *Dans la salle à manger, une horloge Louis XIV au-dessus d'un canapé Napoléon III. Les murs sont tapissés de tissu Bracquenié.* **En haut :** *Bronislaw Krzysztof a créé la table qui représente la chute d'Icare.*

Vorhergehende Seiten: *Die grüne Farbe ist von der Vertäfelung in Versailles inspiriert. Die Krokodilstühle sind von Claude Lalanne, und die Vogelskulptur stammt von César.* **Gegenüberliegende Seite:** *Eine Louis-XIV-Uhr hängt über einem Napoléon-III-Sofa im Esszimmer. Die Wände sind mit Bracquenié-Stoffen bespannt.* **Oben:** *Bronislaw Krzysztof schuf den Tisch, der den Fall des Ikarus symbolisiert.*

Raffaele Curi is a man of the theatre. He has worked as an actor and is now a director. As a sideline, he has also decorated several residences for Alda Fendi, of the famous Roman fur family. Among them is her Parisian apartment, situated in a former artist's studio in Saint-Germain-des-Prés. Fendi says she gave Curi "military instructions" and requested "a rarefied scent of the past in an ultra-modern atmosphere". He translated the brief in a radical fashion and dotted the minimalistic space with artistic references. There was already some paint splattered on the floorboards and he added more. He placed a huge ladder with paint pots on it in the centre of the living room and integrated a collection assembled by Dino Pedriali of photos of Man Ray. "They are really dear to me," asserts Fendi. "For me, Man Ray... is still the artist who best sums up our era."

Alda Fendi

Raffaele Curi est un homme de théâtre, un acteur passé à la mise en scène. Occasionnellement, il décore également les résidences d'Alda Fendi, de la famille des célèbres fourreurs romains, dont son appartement parisien, un atelier d'artiste à Saint-Germain-des-Prés. Pour ce dernier, elle lui a donné « des instructions martiales : un parfum précieux du passé dans une ambiance ultramoderne. » Il s'est attelé à sa mission de manière radicale en parsemant l'espace minimaliste de références artistiques. Il a rajouté des éclaboussures de peinture sur le plancher déjà taché et placé une immense échelle ornée de pots de peinture au centre du séjour. Il y a également intégré une série de portraits de Man Ray par le photographe Dino Pedriali. « J'y tiens beaucoup », confie Fendi. « Pour moi, Man Ray... est encore l'artiste qui résume le mieux notre époque. »

Raffaele Curi ist ein Theatermann. Er hat als Schauspieler gearbeitet und ist jetzt Regisseur. Als Nebenjob hat er außerdem verschiedene Wohnsitze für Alda Fendi, die Tochter aus der berühmten römischen Leder- und Pelzfamilie, eingerichtet. Dazu gehört auch ihr Pariser Appartement, das sich in einem früheren Künstleratelier im Viertel Saint-Germain-des-Prés befindet. Fendi sagt, sie habe Curi »militärische Instruktionen« erteilt und »einen Hauch Vergangenheit in einer ultramodernen Atmosphäre« verlangt. Er befolgte die Anordnung radikal und verteilte in dem minimalistischen Raum zahlreiche Verweise auf die Kunst. Auf den Dielenbrettern prangten bereits mehrere Farbspritzer, denen er weitere hinzufügte. Er stellte eine riesige Leiter mit Farbdosen in die Mitte des Wohnzimmers. Dort integrierte er auch eine Sammlung von Man-Ray-Fotos von Dino Pedriali. »An ihr hänge ich wirklich sehr«, bekräftigt Fendi. »Für mich ist Man Ray ... immer noch der Künstler, der unsere Zeit am besten zusammenfasst.«

Paper designer Eliane Fiévet loves white. When she creates cards and envelopes, the only other colours she uses are silver and gold. The apartment where she has lived since 1961 is equally nuanced and monochromatic. Situated near the Tuileries Gardens, it was built in the Directoire style. She kept all of the period features, such as the mouldings and fireplaces, and adopted a resolutely minimalistic décor. The living room is dominated by the first two prototypes of Shiro Kuramata's famous "How High The Moon" chair. There are also a Dutch chest and English chairs in the master bedroom, and an old desk from a post office in Fiévet's atelier. Her aesthetic, she says, was influenced by her late husband, the Japanese architect Masakazu Bokura. "He taught me how to pare things down and there's been no going back!"

Eliane Fiévet

Créatrice de papier, Eliane Fiévet adore le blanc. Pour ses cartes et enveloppes, les seules autres couleurs qu'elle utilise sont l'or et l'argent. L'appartement qu'elle habite depuis 1961 est pareillement nuancé et monochrome. Son immeuble, situé près des Tuileries, date du Directoire. Elle a conservé les détails d'époque tels que moulures et cheminées, qui ponctuent un décor minimaliste. Son séjour est dominé par les deux premiers prototypes du célèbre fauteuil de Shiro Kuramata « How High The Moon ». Un coffre hollandais et des chaises anglaises meublent sa chambre ; pour son atelier, elle a trouvé un vieux bureau de postier. Elle avoue que son sens esthétique tient beaucoup de son défunt mari, l'architecte japonais Masakazu Bokura. « C'est lui qui m'a appris à dépouiller. Maintenant, c'est irréversible. »

Die Papierdesignerin Eliane Fiévet liebt die Farbe Weiß. Wenn sie Briefkarten und Umschläge entwirft, verwendet sie ansonsten nur noch Silber und Gold. Das Appartement, in dem sie seit 1961 wohnt, ist ebenso monochrom. Es liegt ganz in der Nähe der Tuilerien und wurde im Directoire-Stil erbaut. Sie behielt alle Stilmerkmale der damaligen Zeit wie den Stuck und die Kamine bei, verlegte sich aber auf eine streng minimalistische Einrichtung. Das Wohnzimmer beherrschen die beiden ersten Prototypen von Shiro Kuramatas berühmtem Stuhl »How High The Moon«. Im Schlafzimmer gibt es dafür eine niederländische Kommode und englische Stühle, während in Fiévets Atelier ein alter Schreibtisch aus einem Postamt steht. Ihre Ästhetik, so Fiévet, wurde von ihrem verstorbenen Mann, dem japanischen Architekten Masakazu Bokura beeinflusst. »Er hat mir gezeigt, wie man reduziert, und jetzt gibt es kein Zurück mehr!«

Previous pages: *A view from the living room into the master bedroom. On the wall is a garland from Tsé & Tsé. Beneath it, a paper vase by Pierre Pozzi stands on a zinc box designed by Christine Goumot.*
Above: *A panel of greetings cards created by Fiévet hangs above the bed.*
Right: *Japanese ceramics are arranged on the table in the dining room. The altuglas screen in front of the window was made by Marc Couturier.*

Pages précédentes : *La chambre principale, vue depuis le séjour. Au mur, une guirlande lumineuse de Tsé & Tsé. Dessous, un vase en papier de Pierre Pozzi sur une boîte en zinc de Christine Goumot.*
En haut : *Au-dessus du lit, un panneau de cartes de vœux créées par Fiévet.*
À droite : *Sur la table de la salle à manger, une série de vases japonais en céramique. L'écran en altuglas devant la fenêtre est de Marc Couturier.*

Vorhergehende Seiten: *Ein Blick vom Wohn- ins Schlafzimmer. An der Wand hängt eine Girlande von Tsé & Tsé. Darunter steht eine Papiervase von Pierre Pozzi auf einer Zinkkiste, die Christine Goumot entwarf.*
Oben: *Ein Glasrahmen mit Fiévet-Glückwunschkarten hängt über dem Bett.*
Rechts: *Japanische Keramik wurde auf dem Esszimmertisch arrangiert. Die Altuglas-Sichtblende vor dem Fenster stammt von Marc Couturier.*

Right: In the sitting room, Hans Coray's "Landi" chair stands in front of a Quart de Poil cardboard desk.
Below: In the master bedroom, a Niki de Saint Phalle sculpture stands atop a vintage Dutch chest of drawers. To the left of the fireplace is an Issey Miyake shirt mounted between two sheets of Plexiglas. To the right, an English chair from the late 18-century.
Following pages: Fiévet bought the two Shiro Kuramata prototype chairs in Tokyo. They have solid metal feet, unlike the edited versions. Above the fireplace are a series of her artworks in paper entitled "Figures de Papier".

À droite : Dans le petit salon, une chaise « Landi » d'Hans Coray, devant un bureau en carton de Quart de Poil.
En bas : Dans la chambre principale, une sculpture de Niki de Saint-Phalle posée sur une commode ancienne hollandaise. Sur la gauche de la cheminée, une chemise d'Issey Miyake monté entre deux plaques de plexiglas. Sur sa droite, une chaise anglaise de la fin du XVIIIᵉ siècle.
Pages suivantes : Fiévet a acheté les deux prototypes de Shiro Kuramata à Tokyo. Contrairement aux versions éditées, les fauteuils ont des pieds solides en métal. Au-dessus de la cheminée, une série d'œuvres de la maîtresse de maison intitulées « Figures de Papier ».

Rechts: Im Wohnzimmer steht Hans Corays »Landi«-Stuhl vor einem Papptisch von Quart de Poil.
Unten: Auf einer alten niederländischen Schubladenkommode steht eine Skulptur von Niki de Saint Phalle. Links vom Kamin wurde ein Hemd von Issey Miyake zwischen zwei Plexiglasscheiben montiert. Rechts davon befindet sich ein englischer Stuhl aus dem 18. Jahrhundert.
Folgende Seiten: Fiévet erwarb die beiden Stuhl-Prototypen von Shiro Kuramata in Tokio. Anders als das Serienmodell besitzen sie stabile Metallfüße. Über dem Kamin hängt eine Serie ihrer Papierarbeiten mit dem Titel »Figures de Papier«.

Designer Didier Gomez's apartment in the Marais district used to be home to a pharmaceuticals factory. When he first saw it, the windows were blocked up and there was machinery everywhere. He kept the general floor plan, but removed the glass roof from one of the rooms to create a 300-square-metre garden. "It's like a really peaceful enclave," he asserts. Inside, the interior is peppered with numerous artefacts from Africa – a continent he knows well. Among them is a leather-clad panel that used to grace the wall of a hair salon in Kenya. The hues throughout are deliberately soothing – pistachio for the daytime rooms and chocolate brown for the nocturnal zone. "I work here quite a lot and need a serene space," he explains. He even ended up getting rid of a bright-red Jean Prouvé desk which he used to own. "I just couldn't concentrate with such a striking colour!"

Didier Gomez

L'appartement de Didier Gomez dans le Marais était autrefois une usine pharmaceutique. Quand il l'a visitée la première fois, elle était remplie de machines et les fenêtres étaient condamnées. Il a conservé le plan au sol mais a enlevé la verrière d'une des pièces pour créer un jardin de 300 mètres carrés. « Il est calme. C'est une vraie enclave. » L'intérieur est parsemé d'objets d'Afrique, un continent qu'il connaît bien. Parmi eux, un panneau en cuir qui ornait autrefois un salon de coiffure au Kenya. Partout, les tons sont délibérément apaisants : pistache pour les pièces de jour, chocolat pour la partie nocturne. « Je travaille beaucoup chez moi et j'ai besoin d'un espace serein », explique-t-il. Il s'est même défait de son bureau de Jean Prouvé rouge vif. « Avec cette couleur, je ne pouvais pas me concentrer du tout ! »

In der Wohnung des Designers Didier Gomez im Marais war früher eine Pharmafabrik untergebracht. Als er sie das erste Mal sah, waren die Fenster vernagelt, und überall standen Maschinen herum. Er behielt den ursprünglichen Grundriss bei, ließ aber das Glasdach von einem der Zimmer entfernen, um einen 300 Quadratmeter großen Garten zu schaffen. »Er ist eine wirklich friedliche Oase«, bestätigt er. In der Wohnung sorgen verschiedene Kunstwerke aus Afrika für Abwechslung – ein Kontinent, den Gomez gut kennt. Dazu gehört auch ein Lederpaneel, das einst die Wand eines Friseursalons in Kenia schmückte. Die Farbtöne sind bewusst beruhigend gewählt – Pistazie für die tagsüber benutzten Zimmer und Schokoladenbraun für die Schlafräume. »Ich arbeite oft hier und brauche einen ruhigen Ort«, so der Designer. Deshalb trennte er sich sogar von einem roten Tisch von Jean Prouvé. »Ich konnte mich bei dieser Knallfarbe einfach nicht konzentrieren!«

Previous pages: *A view from the dining room into the kitchen. The column in the corner originally belonged to an English palace.*
Above and right: *The sitting room is dominated by a number of Gomez's own creations, most notably the L-shaped "Opium" sofa (Cinna) and the "Prisme" coffee table (Ligne Roset). The Jérôme Abel Seguin artwork on the wall is made from woven wood fibres.*

Pages précédentes : *Une vue de la cuisine depuis la salle à manger. La colonne dans le coin vient d'un château anglais.*
En haut et à droite : *Dans le salon, de nombreuses créations de Gomez, dont le sofa « Opium » en L (Cinna) et la table basse « Prisme » (Ligne Roset). L'œuvre de Jérôme Abel Seguin au mur est réalisée en tissage de fibres de bois.*

Vorhergehende Seiten: *Blick vom Esszimmer auf die Küche. Die Säule in der Ecke gehörte ursprünglich zu einem englischen Schloss.*
Oben und rechts: *Das Wohnzimmer wird von Gomez' Eigenkreationen beherrscht. Mit am Auffälligsten sind das L-förmige »Opium«-Sofa (Cinna) und der Couchtisch »Prisme« (Ligne Roset). Das Bild an der Wand ist von Jérôme Abel Seguin und besteht aus miteinander verwebten Holzfasern.*

Right: In the office-cum-TV room, two of Gomez's "Annaba" sofas (Ligne Roset) flank an oil painting by Emile Baez. The occasional table in the middle is by Jean-Michel Frank.
Below: In the sitting room, a pony-skin Pascal Mourgue chair stands to the left of Pierre Paulin's "Ribbon" chair.
Following pages: Among the artefacts in the flat are a mask from the Congo and a stool from Mali. The two drawings were executed by Boullard-Devé during André Citroën's "Croisière Jaune" expedition in 1931. The leather panel above the bed originally hung in a hair salon in Kenya.

À droite : Dans le bureau/salle de télévision, deux canapés « Annaba » de Gomez pour Ligne Roset flanquent une huile d'Emile Baez. La table d'appoint au centre est de Jean-Michel Frank.
En bas : Dans le séjour, un siège en poulain de Pascal Mourgue à gauche d'un fauteuil « Ribbon » de Pierre Paulin.
Pages suivantes : Parmi les objets de l'appartement, un masque du Congo et un tabouret malien. Les deux dessins ont été réalisés par Boullard-Devé durant la Croisière Jaune d'André Citroën en 1931. Le panneau en cuir au-dessus du lit vient d'un salon de coiffure kenyan.

Rechts: Im Arbeits- und Fernsehzimmer flankieren Gomez' »Annaba«-Sofas (Ligne Roset) ein Ölgemälde von Emile Baez. Das Beistelltischchen in der Mitte ist von Jean-Michel Frank.
Unten: Im Wohnzimmer steht ein Ponyfell-Sessel von Pascal Mourgue neben Pierre Paulins »Ribbon«-Stuhl.
Folgende Seiten: Zu den Kunstgegenständen in der Wohnung zählen eine Maske aus dem Kongo und ein Hocker aus Mali. Die beiden Zeichnungen fertigte Boullard-Devé 1931 auf der Citroën-Expedition »Croisière Jaune« an. Das Lederpaneel über dem Bett hing in einem Friseursalon in Kenia.

"I can't live without colour," affirms Michelle Halard. "For me, it's essential." Bright hues certainly dominate the 120-square-metre apartment she shares with her husband right by the church of Saint-Sulpice. The dining room is purple, the sitting room green and the bedroom an orangey-red. The couple have been in the interiors business since 1950 and are best known for the furnishings they create under the Yves Halard label. Michelle has also outfitted restaurants and hotels, and created dinnerware for Gien. Here, their decorating approach was free and easy. "It's simply jam-packed with things," admits Michelle. Among them are numerous objects of whimsy – a model of a Danish boat, chairs from a stage set and a wooden figure from a 19th-century merry-go-round.

Michelle & Yves Halard

« Je ne peux pas vivre sans couleurs. Elles me sont vitales », affirme Michelle Halard. De fait, les 120 mètres carrés du couple, à deux pas de l'église Saint-Sulpice, sont dominés par les tons vifs : la salle à manger est violette, le salon vert et la chambre rouge orangé. Ils travaillent dans la décoration depuis 1950 et sont surtout connus pour le mobilier qu'ils créent pour la marque Yves Halard. Michelle a également décoré des hôtels et des restaurants, et dessiné de la vaisselle pour Gien. Dans leur appartement, ils ont opté pour un décor décontracté et facile à vivre. « Un vrai bric-à-brac », reconnaît-elle. On y trouve de nombreux objets coup de cœur : une maquette de bateau danois, des chaises de théâtre et une figure en bois provenant d'un manège du XIXᵉ siècle.

»Ich kann nicht ohne Farbe leben«, bestätigt Michelle Halard. »Sie ist für mich ganz wesentlich.« So wird die 120 Quadratmeter große Wohnung direkt neben der Kirche Saint-Sulpice, die sie gemeinsam mit ihrem Mann bewohnt, eher von kräftigen Farbtönen dominiert. Das Esszimmer ist lila, das Wohnzimmer grün und das Schlafzimmer orangerot. Das Paar ist bereits seit 1950 im Interior-Design-Bereich tätig und vor allem für seine Möbel, die es unter dem Label Yves Halard entwirft, bekannt. Michelle hat auch Restaurants und Hotels ausgestattet sowie Geschirr für Gien entworfen. Bei sich zu Hause sind die beiden ganz locker und unverkrampft an die Einrichtung herangegangen. »Die Wohnung ist einfach mit allem Möglichen vollgestopft«, gibt Michelle zu. Unter anderem mit viel Heiterem, wie dem Modell eines dänischen Boots, Stühlen aus einem Theaterfundus und einer Holzfigur von einem Karussell aus dem 19. Jahrhundert.

Previous pages: The apartment looks out directly onto the church of Saint-Sulpice. Throughout, the flat is filled with a whole host of unusual objects, such as a sculpture from a 19th-century fairground, a wooden Pinocchio and a Chinese horse.
Facing page: A 1930s vase in hammered silver.
Above: A neo-Gothic cabinet dominates the dining room. The dining chairs are the "Clarisse" model from Yves Halard.
Right: A yellow armchair from the Yves Halard collection.

Pages précédentes : Les fenêtres donnent sur l'église Saint-Sulpice. L'appartement est rempli d'objets inhabituels : une sculpture provenant d'une fête foraine du XIXᵉ siècle, un Pinocchio et un cheval chinois.
Page de gauche : Un vase en argent martelé des années 1930.
En haut : Un vaisselier néogothique domine la salle à manger. Les chaises « Clarisse » sont d'Yves Halard.
À droite : Dans le salon, un fauteuil jaune de la collection Yves Halard.

Vorhergehende Seiten: Von der Wohnung sieht man direkt auf die Kirche Saint-Sulpice. Die ganze Wohnung ist voller ungewöhnlicher Objekte: Eine Jahrmarktsfigur aus dem 19. Jahrhundert, ein hölzerner Pinocchio und ein chinesisches Pferd.
Gegenüberliegende Seite: Eine Vase der 1930er-Jahre aus gehämmertem Silber, die die Halards vor etwa 50 Jahren kauften.
Oben: Ein neugotischer Schrank beherrscht das Esszimmer. Die Esszimmerstühle sind das Modell »Clarisse« von Yves Halard.
Rechts: Ein gelber Sessel aus der Yves-Halard-Kollektion steht im Wohnzimmer. Das Gemälde über dem Kamin ist von Christian d'Orgeix.

Previous pages: *Two orange Louis XVI armchairs stand in front of the living-room windows. The rug was created by blowing up the pattern of an Yves Halard fabric. The Yves Halard sofa is upholstered in a cotton velvet from Nobilis and the 18th-century prie-dieu in a yellow damask. The photo with a view from the Casa Malaparte in Capri was taken by the Halards' son, François.*
Above and right: *Michelle often works on her new fabric collections at the kitchen table.*

Pages précédentes : *Deux fauteuils Louis XVI orange devant les fenêtres du salon. Le dessin du tapis est un agrandissement d'un motif de tissu Yves Halard. Le canapé Yves Halard est tapissé d'un velours de coton Nobilis et le prie-Dieu du XVIIIe siècle d'un damas jaune. La vue depuis la maison de Malaparte à Capri est une photo du fils des Halard, François.*
En haut et à droite : *Sur la table de la cuisine, Michelle travaille à sa nouvelle collection de tissus.*

Vorhergehende Seiten: *Zwei orangefarbene Louis-XVI-Sessel stehen vor den Wohnzimmerfenstern. Der Teppich entstand durch die Vergrößerung des Musters eines Yves-Halard-Bezugstoffs. Das Yves-Halard-Sofa ist mit Baumwollsamt von Nobilis bezogen und der Betstuhl aus dem 18. Jahrhundert mit gelbem Damast. Das Foto, das einen Ausblick von der Casa Malaparte auf Capri zeigt, wurde von François, dem Sohn der Halards, aufgenommen.*
Oben und rechts: *Michelle arbeitet oft am Küchentisch an ihren neuen Stoffkollektionen.*

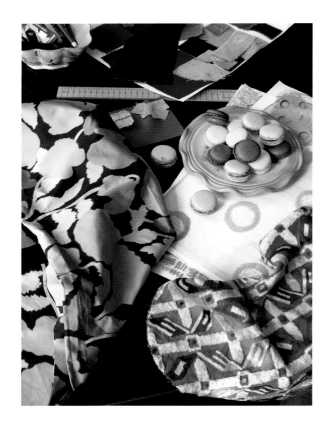

Right: *The armchair was originally made for a theatre production.*
Below: *Above the bed, a female nude by Bernard Dufour.*

À droite : *Ce fauteuil a été conçu pour un décor de théâtre.*
En bass : *Au-dessus du lit, un nu féminin de Bernard Dufour.*

Rechts: *Der Sessel wurde ursprünglich für eine Theateraufführung angefertigt.*
Unten: *Über dem Bett hängt eine Arbeit von Bernard Dufour, die einen weiblichen Akt zeigt.*

Fashion designer Anne Valérie Hash must have one of the most spectacular showrooms in existence. Its main room shimmers with thousands of tiny gold mosaics and boasts both ornately painted ceilings and a whole host of wonderfully bizarre sculptures. In the 19th century, it was part of a restaurant called "Marguery", frequented by the likes of Émile Zola. Its history since then has been equally colourful. It has successively been a brothel, a synagogue and the headquarters of a strange African sect. When Hash first saw it, there was "monstrous" red carpet everywhere, a tasteless mirrored drop ceiling and hundreds of pigeons. With the help of architect Isabelle Stanislas, she got everything in shape in just five weeks! The result is simply bewitching. As Hash herself says, "Something attracted me to the place, like a magnet."

Anne Valérie Hash

Le showroom de la styliste Anne Valérie Hash est tout simplement spectaculaire. Sa pièce principale est ornée de milliers de petites mosaïques dorées chatoyantes, de plafonds peints et ouvragés, de sculptures merveilleusement bizarres. Au XIXᵉ siècle, il faisait partie d'un restaurant, le Marguery, dont Émile Zola était l'un des piliers. Depuis, il a connu une histoire pittoresque, ayant été maison close, synagogue puis quartier général d'une étrange secte africaine. Lorsque Hash l'a découvert, il y avait partout une moquette rouge « monstrueuse », un faux-plafond en miroir d'un goût douteux et des centaines de pigeons. Avec l'architecte Isabelle Stanislas, elles l'ont restauré en cinq semaines seulement ! Le résultat est envoûtant. Comme le dit Hash elle-même : « Quelque chose m'a attiré ici, comme un aimant. »

Die Modedesignerin Anne Valérie Hash besitzt einen der spektakulärsten Showrooms überhaupt. Der Hauptraum, in dem Tausende von winzigen Goldmosaiken um die Wette schimmern, prunkt mit bemalten Kassettendecken und beherbergt wunderbar bizarre Skulpturen. Im 19. Jahrhundert gehörte er zu einem Restaurant namens »Marguery«, das von Berühmtheiten wie Émile Zola besucht wurde. Seine anschließende Geschichte ist nicht weniger faszinierend. Er war nacheinander Bordell, Synagoge und schließlich das Hauptquartier einer abstrusen afrikanischen Sekte. Als ihn Hash das erste Mal sah, lag überall ein »monströser« roter Teppich. Es gab eine geschmacklose, abgehängte Spiegeldecke sowie Hunderte von Tauben. Mithilfe der Architektin Isabelle Stanislas gelang es ihr in nur fünf Wochen, alles auf Vordermann zu bringen! Das Ergebnis ist einfach betörend. Hash sagt selbst: »Irgendwie hat mich der Ort angezogen wie ein Magnet.«

Previous pages: Jurgen Bey's "Light Shade Shade" chandelier illuminates the Flemish Room. The Jeppe Hein electrical installation is entitled "Neon Cube 90°".
Above: Some of Hash's fashion creations stand at the top of the main staircase.
Right: The velvet sofa was found at Montreuil flea market.
Facing page: Hash stocks her former collections on the gallery, which was added to the Flemish Room in the 1960s.
Following pages: The letters on the fireplace spell out "Marguery" – the name of the 19th-century restaurant.

Pages précédentes : Un lustre de Jurgen Bey, « Light Shade Shade », illumine la salle flamande. L'installation électrique de Jeppe Hein s'intitule « Neon Cube 90° ».
En haut : Des modèles de Hash attendent en haut des escaliers.
À droite : Le canapé rouge a été trouvé aux Puces de Montreuil.
Page de droite : Hash stocke ses anciennes collections sur la mezzanine, ajoutée à la salle flamande dans les années 1960.
Pages suivantes : Sur la cheminée, l'enseigne du « Marguery », le restaurant du XIXᵉ siècle pour lequel la salle flamande a été conçue.

Vorhergehende Seiten: Jurgen Beys »Light Shade Shade«-Kronleuchter erhellt das Flämische Zimmer. Die Lichtinstallation auf dem Boden von Jeppe Hein heißt »Neon Cube 90°«.
Oben: Einige von Hashs Modekreationen stehen am Ende des großen Treppenaufgangs.
Rechts: Das rote Samtsofa stammt vom Flohmarkt in Montreuil.
Gegenüberliegende Seite: Hash bewahrt ihre früheren Kollektionen auf der Galerie auf, die in den 1960er-Jahren hinzugefügt wurde.
Folgende Seiten: Die Buchstaben auf dem Kamin bilden das Wort »Marguery« – so hieß das Restaurant im 19. Jahrhundert.

Swiss-born attorney-at-law Martin Hatebur bought his first work of art (an untitled piece by Christopher Wool) in 1996. Today, it hangs in his Paris living room. The front of the two-floor flat looks out directly over the Seine. At the back, the kitchen is housed in what was originally a winter garden built by Gustave Eiffel. Hatebur says it took him about ten years to furnish. Over that time, he has accumulated every light created by his designer friend, Arik Levy, as well as numerous pieces by Charlotte Perriand, Jean Prouvé and Pierre Jeanneret. Still, his main passion remains art. He talks about discovering Polish painter Wilhelm Sasnal on a trip to Warsaw and admits to having some 100 works divided between Paris and his home in Basle.

Martin Hatebur

L'avocat suisse Martin Hatebur a acheté sa première œuvre d'art en 1996 (un Christopher Wool sans titre). Aujourd'hui, elle est accrochée dans son séjour parisien. La façade du duplex donne sur la Seine ; à l'arrière, sa cuisine est située dans un ancien jardin d'hiver construit par Gustave Eiffel. Hatebur a mis dix ans à le meubler. Durant cette période, il a accumulé tous les luminaires créés par son ami Arik Levy ainsi que de nombreuses pièces de Charlotte Perriand, Jean Prouvé et Pierre Jeanneret. Mais l'art demeure sa vraie passion. Il raconte comment il a découvert le peintre polonais Wilhelm Sasnal lors d'un séjour à Varsovie et avoue posséder près de 100 œuvres réparties entre Paris et sa demeure à Bâle.

Der in der Schweiz geborene Rechtsanwalt Martin Hatebur erwarb sein erstes Kunstwerk 1996 (eine Arbeit von Christopher Wool ohne Titel). Heute hängt es in seinem Pariser Wohnzimmer. Der Blick aus der über zwei Geschosse reichenden Wohnung geht direkt auf die Seine hinaus. Die auf der Hofseite liegende Küche befindet sich in einem früheren Wintergarten, der von Gustave Eiffel gebaut wurde. Hatebur meint, er habe gut zehn Jahre zum Einrichten gebraucht. In dieser Zeit sammelte er jede Lampe seines Freundes, des Designers Arik Levy, sowie zahlreiche Möbel von Charlotte Perriand, Jean Prouvé und Pierre Jeanneret. Trotzdem gilt seine größte Liebe der Kunst. Er erzählt davon, wie er auf einer Warschaureise den polnischen Künstler Wilhelm Sasnal entdeckte, und gesteht, in seinen Wohnungen in Paris und Basel bestimmt 100 Kunstwerke zu besitzen.

Previous pages: Verner Panton's "Flower Pot" light fixture hangs above a monastery table in the dining room next to a light box by Chen Zhen. The kitchen features a Piet Hein and Bruno Mathsson table, Jean Prouvé "Standard" chairs, Arik Levy's "Flexible Flyer" ceiling light, and artworks by Wilhelm Sasnal (left) and Georgine Ingold (right).
Right: Above a Charlotte Perriand/Ateliers Jean Prouvé bookshelf in the office is a work by Sigmar Polke.
Below: In the living room, an untitled work by Christopher Wool as well as two photos by Ryan Gander hang behind a sofa from the store Caravane in Paris.

Pages précédentes : Dans la salle à manger, un lustre « Flower Pot » de Verner Panton est suspendu au-dessus d'une table de monastère. Au sol, une boîte lumineuse de Chen Zhen. Dans la cuisine, une table de Piet Hein et Bruno Mathsson, des chaises « Standard » de Jean Prouvé, un plafonnier « Flexible Flyer » d'Arik Levy et des œuvres d'art de Wilhelm Sasnal (à gauche) et de Georgine Ingold (à droite).
À droite : Dans le bureau, au-dessus des étagères de Charlotte Perriand pour les ateliers Jean Prouvé, une œuvre de Sigmar Polke.
En bas : Dans le séjour, une œuvre sans titre de Christopher Wool ainsi que deux photos de Ryan Gander sont accrochées derrière un canapé provenant de la boutique Caravane à Paris.

Vorhergehende Seiten: Verner Pantons »Flower Pot«-Lampen hängen über einem Refektoriumstisch im Esszimmer neben einem Leucht-kasten von Chen Zhen. In der Küche kann man einen Tisch von Piet Hein und Bruno Mathsson, »Standard«-Stühle von Jean Prouvé, Arik Levys »Flexible Flyer«-Deckenleuchte sowie Kunst von Wilhelm Sasnal (links) und Georgine Ingold (rechts) bewundern.
Rechts: Über dem Bücherregal von Charlotte Perriand, Ateliers Jean Prouvé, hängt eine Arbeit von Sigmar Polke.
Unten: Im Wohnzimmer hängen eine Arbeit von Christopher Wool sowie zwei Fotografien von Ryan Gander hinter einem Sofa aus dem Geschäft »Caravane« in Paris.

Above: The desk was designed by Arne Vodder and the sofas by Pierre Jeanneret for Chandigarh in India.
Right: The master bedroom is situated on the top floor of the duplex.
Following pages: The living room is decorated with artworks by Christopher Wool (left), Stephen Prina (right) and two small works by Ugo Rondinone (far right). There is also a Charlotte Perriand stool and a bench, which she created for the Cité Cansado in Mauritania for a firm called Miferma. In the background is Jean Prouvé's "Antony" daybed.

En haut : Un bureau d'Arne Vodder. Les canapés ont été dessinés par Pierre Jeanneret pour Chandigarh en Inde.
À droite : La chambre principale se trouve au deuxième étage du duplex.
Pages suivantes : Dans le séjour, des œuvres de Christopher Wool (à gauche), Stephen Prina et deux petits tableaux d'Ugo Rondinone (à droite) ; un tabouret de Charlotte Perriand et un banc qu'elle a dessiné pour la Cité Cansado de la société mauritanienne Miferma. Au fond, un lit de repos « Antony » de Jean Prouvé.

Oben: Der Schreibtisch stammt von Arne Vodder, und die Sofas sind ein Entwurf von Pierre Jeanneret für Chandigarh in Indien.
Rechts: Das Schlafzimmer befindet sich im oberen Geschoss der Duplexwohnung.
Folgende Seiten: Im Wohnzimmer sieht man Kunst von Christopher Wool (links), Stephen Prina und zwei kleine Arbeiten von Ugo Rondinone (rechts). Eine Bank von Charlotte Perriand für Miferma, Cité Cansado, Mauretanien, dient als Sofatisch, der Hocker ist ebenfalls von Perriand und die »Antony«-Liege von Jean Prouvé.

THAT WOULD HAVE BEEN WONDERFUL

ANDRO WEKUA & EDITION PATRICK FREY

CHRISTOPHER WOOL

If modernity is a question of mixing styles, then this apartment is certainly of its time. For its former occupants, Jacques Garcia created an ornate, neo-Gothic décor. There are 19th-century fabrics on the walls, rich colours and kitchen cupboards made from the wood panelling of an old chapel. The master bathroom, meanwhile, is kitted out with a throne from a St. Petersburg palace and antique Roman onyx. The present owner has changed very little. He has even kept the curtains and some of his predecessors' old-style furniture. He did, however, bring with him an exceptional collection of 20th-century design pieces by Jean Royère, Gaetano Pesce and the like. It took about two years for everything to find its place. Now that it has, it looks perfectly at home. As the owner says, "The mix may be daring, but it's also extremely harmonious".

Boulevard Haussmann

Si la modernité appelle un mélange de styles, cet appartement reflète bien l'esprit de son temps. Jacques Garcia a créé pour ses anciens occupants un riche décor néogothique : teintures murales du XIXᵉ siècle, couleurs opulentes, placards de cuisine réalisés avec les boiseries d'une ancienne chapelle... Il y a même un trône venu d'un palais de Saint-Pétersbourg et de l'onyx de la Rome antique dans la salle de bains principale. Le nouveau propriétaire n'a pratiquement rien touché, conservant même les rideaux et certains meubles. En revanche, il a apporté avec lui son exceptionnelle collection de design du XXᵉ siècle, dont des pièces de Jean Royère et de Gaetano Pesce. Il a fallu deux ans avant que chaque objet trouve sa place, mais à présent, comme il le dit lui-même, « le mélange est peut-être audacieux mais aussi très harmonieux ».

Wenn Modernität bedeutet, Stile zu mischen, ist diese Wohnung mit Sicherheit zeitgemäß. Für ihre vorherigen Bewohner schuf Jacques Garcia ein opulentes, neugotisches Dekor. Es gibt Stofftapeten aus dem 19. Jahrhundert, leuchtende Farben und Küchenschränke, die aus der Holzvertäfelung einer alten Kapelle gefertigt wurden. Das Bad ist mit einem Thron aus einem St. Petersburger Palast ausgestattet sowie mit antikem, römischem Onyx. Der heutige Eigentümer hat daran nur wenig verändert. Er behielt sogar die Vorhänge bei sowie einige Stilmöbel seines Vorgängers. Dafür brachte er eine außergewöhnliche Sammlung von Designerstücken des 20. Jahrhunderts mit – Objekte von Jean Royère, Gaetano Pesce und anderen. Es dauerte zwei Jahre, bis alles seinen Platz fand, aber jetzt ist es perfekt. »Die Mischung mag mutig sein, ist aber auch extrem harmonisch«, so der Besitzer.

Previous pages: In the entrance hall, a suite of Jean Royère furniture is arranged around a coffee table designed by Charlotte Perriand and Jean Prouvé. The dog is a work by Jeff Koons. **Above:** *An Ettore Sottsass bookshelf stands at the bottom of the stairs, which lead up to the bedrooms.* **Facing page:** *A mix of the new and old in the sitting room – two 19th-century armchairs, a Charlotte Perriand bench and two works of art by Alain Séchas, on the fireplace.*

Pages précédentes : Dans le hall d'entrée, un ensemble de sièges de Jean Royère disposés autour d'une table basse de Charlotte Perriand et de Jean Prouvé. Le chien est une œuvre de Jeff Koons. **En haut :** *Des étagères d'Ettore Sottsass au pied de l'escalier qui mène aux chambres.* **Page de droite :** *Dans le salon, un mélange harmonieux d'ancien et de moderne : deux fauteuils du XIXe siècle, un banc de Charlotte Perriand et, sur la cheminée, deux œuvres d'Alain Séchas.*

Vorhergehende Seiten: Im Eingangsbereich wurden Jean-Royère-Möbel um einen Couchtisch von Charlotte Perriand und Jean Prouvé gruppiert. Der Hund ist ein Multiple von Jeff Koons. **Oben:** *Ein Bücherregal von Ettore Sottsass steht am Fuß der Treppe, die zu weiteren Zimmern führt.* **Gegenüberliegende Seite:** *Ein harmonischer Mix von Alt und Neu im Wohnzimmer – zwei Sessel aus dem 19. Jahrhundert, eine Bank von Charlotte Perriand und zwei Arbeiten von Alain Séchas auf dem Kamin.*

Previous double page: A Didier Marcel sculpture of a chocolate grinder stands on the marble coffee table in the dining room. The curvaceous chaise longue in front of it is a creation by Martin Szekely.
Facing page: The neo-Gothic breakfast room is perfectly in tune with the spirit of the apartment.
Left: The kitchen units were made from wood panellings from a chapel. The range is from La Cornue.
Below: A Christian Boltanski sculpture and a Christian de Portzamparc armchair in the dining room.

Double page précédente : Sur la table basse en marbre de la salle à manger, une sculpture de Didier Marcel représentant une broyeuse de chocolat. Devant, une chaise longue arrondie de Martin Szekely.
Page de gauche : La « breakfast room » néogothique s'harmonise parfaitement avec l'esprit de l'appartement.
À gauche : Les placards de la cuisine ont été réalisés avec des boiseries récupérées dans une chapelle. La cuisinière vient de chez La Cornue.
En bas : Dans la salle à manger, une sculpture de Christian Boltanski et un fauteuil de Christian de Portzamparc.

Vorhergehende Doppelseite: Auf dem Marmorcouchtisch im Esszimmer steht die Skulptur einer Schokoladenmühle von Didier Marcel. Die kurvenreiche Chaiselongue im Vordergrund stammt von Martin Szekely.
Gegenüberliegende Seite: Der neugotische Frühstücksraum passt hervorragend zur Atmosphäre der Wohnung.
Links: Die Küchenschränke bestehen aus den Holzvertäfelungen einer Kapelle. Der Herd ist von La Cornue.
Unten: Im Esszimmer finden sich eine Skulptur von Christian Boltanski und ein Sessel von Christian de Portzamparc.

Pages 132/133: In one part of the sitting room, a Prouvé coffee table is juxtaposed with a Napoleon III-style sofa, a golden Philippe Starck stool and a white papier-mâché chair, which the owner found at a flea market. Clockwise from top left: A multicoloured Garouste & Bonetti standing light in the master bedroom. A Prouvé chair and a Perriand bookshelf in the dining room. A throne from a St. Petersburg palace in the master bathroom. A Fabrice Hyber work and Pierre Paulin sofa in the study.

Pages 132/133 : Dans un coin du salon, une table basse de Jean Prouvé devant un canapé de style Napoléon III, un tabouret doré de Philippe Starck et une chaise blanche en papier mâché chinée aux Puces. Depuis en haut à gauche dans le sens des aiguilles d'une montre : dans la chambre de maître, un lampadaire multicolore de Garouste & Bonetti. Dans la salle à manger, un fauteuil de Jean Prouvé et une bibliothèque de Charlotte Perriand. Dans la salle de bains principale, un trône provenant d'un palais de Saint-Pétersbourg. Dans le bureau, une œuvre de Fabrice Hyber au-dessus d'un canapé de Pierre Paulin.

Seiten 132/133: In einem Teil des Wohnzimmers wurde ein Prouvé-Couchtisch mit einem Sofa im Napoléon-III-Stil, einem goldenen Hocker von Philippe Starck sowie einem Stuhl aus weißem Papiermaschee kombiniert, den der Besitzer auf einem Flohmarkt entdeckte. Im Uhrzeigersinn von links: Im Schlafzimmer steht eine bunte Stehlampe von Garouste & Bonetti. Ein Prouvé-Stuhl und ein Perriand-Regal sind im Esszimmer zu sehen. Im Bad gibt es einen Thron aus einem Palast in St. Petersburg. Im Arbeitszimmer befinden sich Kunst von Fabrice Hyber und ein Sofa von Pierre Paulin.

Above: A Jean Royère light fixture hangs above the red velvet head-board in the master bedroom. The religious painting dates from the 18th century.
Right and facing page: The guest room is painted a vivid green. To the left of the door, a George Nelson sofa sits beneath a work by Philippe Perrin entitled "La Panoplie", which incorporates objects used for boxing.

En haut : Dans la chambre principale, un luminaire de Jean Royère est accroché au-dessus de la tête de lit en velours rouge. La peinture religieuse date du XVIIIᵉ siècle.
À droite et page de droite : La chambre d'amis est peinte d'un vert vif. À gauche de la porte, un canapé de George Nelson sous une œuvre de Philippe Perrin incorporant des objets du monde de la boxe et intitulée « La Panoplie ».

Oben: Eine Jean-Royère-Leuchte hängt über dem mit rotem Samt bezogenen Betthaupt im Schlafzimmer. Das religiöse Gemälde stammt aus dem 18. Jahrhundert.
Rechts und gegenüberliegende Seite: Das Gästezimmer ist in einem kräftigen Grün gestrichen. Links von der Tür steht ein Sofa von George Nelson unter einer Arbeit von Philippe Perrin mit dem Titel »La Panoplie«, die Boxzubehör enthält.

When Rome-based architect Cristina Finucci was asked to work on this pied-à-terre in Saint-Germain-des-Prés, she decided to create an interior that would reflect the Italian owners' two great passions: exoticism and travel. The starting point for the décor was the exquisite Chinese lacquer screen, which separates the dining and sitting areas in the main room. In the guest bedroom, Finucci housed the bathroom in a nomadic tent-like structure equipped with a zinc roof and raw-linen curtains. Elsewhere, she incorporated modern classics by the likes of Charlotte Perriand and Ettore Sottsass, and uncovered a series of portrait drawings above the main fireplace, left by a previous occupant. "It used to be an artist's studio," explains Finucci. Further back in the 16th century, the building even housed the British embassy.

Rue Jacob

Quand l'architecte romaine Cristina Finucci s'est attaquée à ce pied-à-terre à Saint-Germain-des-Prés, elle a voulu un décor qui refléterait les deux passions des propriétaires italiens : l'exotisme et les voyages. Elle est partie de l'exquis paravent en laque chinoise qui sépare les coins salon et salle à manger dans la pièce principale. Dans la chambre d'amis, elle a niché une salle de bains sous une « tente nomade » au toit en zinc et protégée de rideaux en lin grège. Ailleurs, elle a intégré des « classiques modernes » de Charlotte Perriand ou d'Ettore Sottsass, et découvert une série de portraits au crayon dessinés par un ancien occupant au-dessus de la cheminée. « Autrefois, c'était un atelier d'artiste », explique-t-elle. Plus loin dans le temps, au XVIe siècle, l'immeuble a également accueilli l'ambassade britannique.

Als die in Rom ansässige Architektin Cristina Finucci gebeten wurde, dieses Pied-à-terre in Saint-Germain-des-Prés einzurichten, beschloss sie, ein Ambiente zu schaffen, das die beiden großen Leidenschaften seiner italienischen Besitzer widerspiegelt: Exotik und Reisen. Dreh- und Angelpunkt war der kostbare chinesische Lack-Paravent, der den Ess- vom Wohnbereich trennt. Im Gästezimmer brachte Finucci das Bad in einer Art Nomadenzelt mit Zinkdach und Vorhängen aus grobem Leinen unter. Dazu kombinierte sie moderne Klassiker von Designern wie Charlotte Perriand und Ettore Sottsass. Außerdem legte sie eine Reihe von Porträtzeichnungen über dem großen Kamin frei, die von einem früheren Bewohner stammen. »Die Wohnung war einmal ein Künstleratelier«, so Finucci. Im 16. Jahrhundert beherbergte das Gebäude sogar die britische Botschaft.

Previous pages: In the sitting room, two Mies van der Rohe "Barcelona" chairs are juxtaposed with a bronze "Marguerites" coffee table by Hubert Le Gall. The owners asked for their portraits to be added to the wooden panel above the fireplace, formerly hidden by a mirror.
Right: In the guest bedroom, Finucci created a tent-like structure to house the bathroom.
Below: The dining table is a prototype designed by Riccardo Rolando. The "Tulip" chairs are by Eero Saarinen.

Pages précédentes : Dans le salon, deux fauteuils « Barcelona » de Mies van der Rohe côtoient une table basse en bronze « Marguerites » d'Hubert Le Gall. Les propriétaires ont tenu à intégrer leurs portraits à ceux dessinés sur la boiserie au-dessus de la cheminée, autrefois cachés par un miroir.
À droite : Dans la chambre d'amis, Finucci a créé une tente pour accueillir la salle de bains.
En bas : La table de la salle à manger est un prototype de Riccardo Rolando. Les chaises « Tulip » sont d'Eero Saarinen.

Vorhergehende Seiten: Im Wohnzimmer kontrastieren zwei »Barcelona«-Sessel von Mies van der Rohe mit einem bronzenen »Marguerites«-Couchtisch von Hubert Le Gall. Die Eigentümer baten darum, dass auch ihre Porträts auf dem Holzpaneel über dem Kamin hinzugefügt werden, das vorher von einem Spiegel verdeckt war.
Rechts: Im Gästezimmer schuf Finucci eine Art Zelt, in dem sich das Bad versteckt.
Unten: Der Esstisch ist ein Prototyp von Riccardo Rolando. Die »Tulip«-Stühle sind von Eero Saarinen.

Above: A standing lamp by the late Italian designer Tony Cordero and
a four-poster bed dominate the master bedroom. The black chair is a
prototype, designed by Philippe Starck for a Parisian nightclub.
Right: Three lithographs by Roy Lichtenstein hang above a laminate
chest created by Charlotte Perriand and Jean Prouvé for the headquarters of Air France.

En haut : Dans la chambre de maître, un lampadaire de feu Tony
Cordero et un lit à baldaquin. Le fauteuil noir est un prototype de
Philippe Stark pour un night-club parisien.
À droite : Trois lithographies de Roy Lichtenstein au-dessus d'un
meuble en laminé créé par Charlotte Perriand et Jean Prouvé pour
le quartier général d'Air France.

Oben: Eine Stehlampe des verstorbenen italienischen Designers Tony
Cordero sowie ein Himmelbett beherrschen das Schlafzimmer. Der
schwarze Stuhl ist ein Prototyp, den Philippe Starck für einen Pariser
Nachtclub entwarf.
Rechts: Drei Lithografien von Roy Lichtenstein hängen über einem
Sideboard, das Charlotte Perriand und Jean Prouvé für die Firmen-
zentrale der Air France schufen.

Philippe Jousse still clearly remembers meeting Jean Prouvé. "He was very open and nice," he asserts. "Much less austere than you'd think." The first piece of design he bought in the late 1970s was an emblematic Prouvé "Compas" table. Since, he's gone on to become one of the world's leading dealers of 20th-century furniture. In Paris, he has three different galleries. One specialises in Prouvé and his contemporaries, another in 1960s and 1970s design, and a third in contemporary art. The 90-square-metre apartment he shares with his wife, Patricia, is certainly filled with some wonderful treasures. Overlooking the Port de l'Arsenal near the Bastille, it was restructured with the help of architects Dominique Marrec and Emmanuel Combarel. Cantilevered stairs lead up to a terrace. "It's really great living on the top floor," he says. Given the spectacular views, there's not much arguing with that!

Patricia & Philippe Jousse

Philippe Jousse se souvient encore de sa rencontre avec Jean Prouvé. « Il était très ouvert et sympathique. Beaucoup moins austère qu'on l'aurait cru. » Le premier meuble design qu'il a acheté à la fin des années 1970 était sa fameuse table « Compas ». Depuis, il est devenu l'un des premiers marchands de design du XXᵉ siècle du monde. Rien qu'à Paris, il possède trois galeries ; la première consacrée à Prouvé, la seconde au design des années 1960 et 1970, et la troisième à l'art contemporain. L'appartement de 90 mètres carrés qu'il partage avec sa femme Patricia est rempli de trésors. Dominant le port de l'Arsenal près de la Bastille, il a été restructuré avec l'aide des architectes Dominique Marrec et Emmanuel Combarel. « Vivre au dernier étage est formidable » confie Jousse.

Philippe Jousse kann sich noch gut daran erinnern, wie er Jean Prouvé kennenlernte. »Er war sehr nett und aufgeschlossen«, bestätigt er. »Gar nicht so unnahbar, wie man glauben würde.« Das erste Möbelstück, das er Ende der 1970er-Jahre von Prouvé kaufte, war dessen beispielhafter »Compas«-Tisch. Seitdem hat Jousse sich zu einem der führenden Händler für Möbel des 20. Jahrhunderts entwickelt. In Paris besitzt er inzwischen drei Galerien. Eine ist auf Prouvé und dessen Zeitgenossen spezialisiert, eine andere auf das Design der 1960er- und 1970er-Jahre und eine dritte auf zeitgenössische Kunst. Die 90 Quadratmeter große Wohnung, die er mit seiner Frau Patricia bewohnt, ist ganz sicher mit zahlreichen Schätzen eingerichtet. Sie gewährt Ausblick auf den Port de l'Arsenal unweit der Bastille und wurde mithilfe der Architekten Dominique Marrec und Emmanuel Combarel renoviert. Eine freitragende Treppe führt hoch zum Dachgarten. »Es ist wirklich toll, im obersten Geschoss zu wohnen«, sagt er. Bei der spektakulären Aussicht kann man ihm nicht widersprechen!

Previous pages: Cantilevered stairs lead up to the roof terrace. One of Jean Prouvé's famous "porthole" panels acts as a divider between the main room and the kitchen.
Right: A ceiling light by Ronan & Erwan Bouroullec hangs above a Ron Arad coffee table.
Below: Beneath the stairs is a chair created by the artist Franz West. The sideboard was created by Pierre Jeanneret and Charlotte Perriand for a scientist in 1945. It is one of only two in existence. The pair of "Kangourou" armchairs meanwhile were made by Jean Prouvé for his friends' holiday villa in the south of France.

Pages précédentes : Un escalier cantilever mène à la terrasse sur le toit. Un des célèbres panneaux « d'Hublot » de Jean Prouvé sépare la salle principale de la cuisine.
À droite : Un plafonnier de Ronan & Erwan Bouroullec suspendu au-dessus d'une table basse de Ron Arad.
En bas : Sous l'escalier, une chaise créée par l'artiste Franz West. Le buffet fut dessiné en 1945 par Pierre Jeanneret et Charlotte Perriand pour un chercheur. Il n'en existe que deux exemplaires. Jean Prouvé conçut la paire de fauteuils « Kangourou » pour la maison de vacances d'amis dans le sud de la France.

Vorhergehende Seiten: Eine freitragende Treppe führt hinauf zum Dachgarten. Eines von Jean Prouvés berühmten »Bullaugen«-Paneelen dient als Raumteiler zwischen Wohnzimmer und Küche.
Rechts: Eine Deckenlampe der Brüder Ronan & Erwan Bouroullec hängt über einem Couchtisch von Ron Arad.
Unten: Unter der Treppe steht ein Stuhl, den der Künstler Franz West gestaltet hat. Das Sideboard wurde 1945 von Pierre Jeanneret und Charlotte Perriand für einen Wissenschaftler entworfen. Es ist eines von nur zwei Exemplaren. Die beiden »Kangourou«-Sessel dagegen wurden von Jean Prouvé für das Feriendomizil von Freunden in Südfrankreich geschaffen.

Above: The Andreas Gursky photo depicts the port of Salerno, Italy. The green cactus is a clothes stand designed by Drocco and Mello in 1972.
Right: The yellow "Molaire" ceramic on the coffee table is a piece by Georges Jouve. The small wooden stools are by Charlotte Perriand.
Following pages: The "Centrale" dining table, the aluminium "Standard" chairs and the "Swing Jib" wall lamp from the Air France building in Congo are all by Prouvé. The Jouve ceramic is called "Calice" and the small drawing on the wall is by Jean-Michel Basquiat.

En haut : Une photo du port de Salerno, en Italie, d'Andreas Gursky. Le cactus est un présentoir de vêtements créé par Drocco et Mello en 1972.
À droite : La « Molaire » en céramique jaune sur la table basse est une œuvre de Georges Jouve. Les petits tabourets en bois sont de Charlotte Perriand.
Pages suivantes : La table « Centrale », les chaises « Standard » en aluminium et le luminaire « Swing Jib » provenant du bâtiment Air France au Congo sont tous de Jean Prouvé. Le vase en céramique « Calice » est de Georges Jouve et le petit dessin au mur de Jean-Michel Basquiat.

Oben: Das Foto von Andreas Gursky zeigt den Hafen von Salerno, Italien. Der grüne Kaktus ist ein Kleiderständer, den Drocco und Mello 1972 entwarfen.
Rechts: Die gelbe »Molaire«-Keramik auf dem Couchtisch ist von Georges Jouve. Die kleinen Holzhocker stammen von Charlotte Perriand.
Folgende Seiten: Der »Centrale«-Esstisch, die »Standard«-Stühle und die »Swing Jib«-Wandleuchte aus dem Air-France-Gebäude im Kongo sind alle von Prouvé. Die Jouve-Keramik heißt »Calice«, und die kleine Zeichnung an der Wand ist von Jean-Michel Basquiat.

Above: In the kitchen, the "Granipoli" table from 1939 is another of Prouvé's creations. On the Boffi kitchen units are a lamp and fruit bowl by Mathieu Matégot, as well as artworks by Philippe Meste incorporating photos of supermodels.
Right: In the guest bathroom, an oil painting by Bernard Frize hangs above two sinks created by the Atelier Van Lieshout.
Facing page: On the far side of the dining table is the famous "Mexique" bookshelf – a collaborative effort between Prouvé and Perriand.

En haut : Dans la cuisine, la table « Granipoli » est une autre création de Jean Prouvé de 1939. Sur les éléments de cuisine Boffi, une lampe et une coupe à fruits de Mathieu Matégot, ainsi que des œuvres d'art de Philippe Meste incorporant des photos de top-modèles.
À droite : Dans la salle de bains des invités, une peinture à l'huile de Bernard Frize au-dessus de lavabos de l'Atelier Van Lieshout.
Page de droite : Derrière la table, la célèbre bibliothèque « Mexique », une œuvre conjointe de Prouvé et Perriand.

Oben: Der »Granipoli«-Tisch in der Küche ist von 1939 und ebenfalls ein Entwurf von Prouvé. Auf der Boffi-Küchenzeile stehen eine Lampe und eine Obstschale von Mathieu Matégot sowie Kunst von Philippe Meste, der Fotos von Supermodels verwendete.
Rechts: Im Gästebad hängt ein Ölbild von Bernard Frize über zwei Waschbecken aus dem Atelier Van Lieshout.
Gegenüberliegende Seite: Hinter dem Esstisch ist das berühmte Bücherregal »Mexique« zu sehen – ein Gemeinschaftsentwurf von Prouvé und Perriand.

Facing page: *A chair that Prouvé created for an amphitheatre stands next to Serge Mouille's "Signal" standing light.*
Above: *In the master bedroom, Perriand's "Ombre" chair sits beneath an artwork by Valentin Carron. The photo is by Erwin Wurm, the bedspread was custom-made by Rick Owens and the wall lamp is by Le Corbusier.*
Right: *The bookshelves are yet another Perriand creation.*

Page de gauche : *Une chaise dessinée par Prouvé pour un amphithéâtre près d'un lampadaire « Signal » de Serge Mouille.*
En haut : *Dans la chambre principale, une chaise « Ombre » de Perriand, sous une œuvre de Valentin Carron. La photo est d'Erwin Wurm. Le dessus-de-lit a été réalisé sur mesure par Rick Owens. L'applique est de Le Corbusier.*
À droite : *Une autre bibliothèque dessinée par Perriand.*

Gegenüberliegende Seite: *Ein Stuhl, den Prouvé für ein Amphitheater entwarf, steht neben der »Signal«-Stehlampe von Serge Mouille.*
Oben: *Im Schlafzimmer befindet sich Perriands »Ombre«-Stuhl unter einem Kunstwerk von Valentin Carron. Das Foto stammt von Erwin Wurm, der Bettüberwurf ist eine Spezialanfertigung von Rick Owens, und die Wandlampe ist von Le Corbusier.*
Rechts: *Die Bücherregale sind wieder ein Entwurf von Perriand.*

Below: The "Copacabana" table and chairs are by Matégot.
Following pages: The view at night, with the Eiffel Tower glittering in the distance, is truly mesmerising.

En bas : La table et les chaises « Copacabana » sont de Matégot.
Pages suivantes : La vue de nuit, avec la tour Eiffel scintillant au loin, est vraiment hypnotique.

Unten: Der »Copacabana«-Tisch und die Stühle sind von Matégot.
Folgende Seiten: Die Aussicht bei Nacht, wenn der Eiffelturm in der Ferne funkelt, ist wirklich hypnotisierend.

Facing page: A view of the apartment building across the Port de l'Arsenal.
Above: On the roof terrace, the Jousses have installed a red stool and an aluminium sun shield created by Prouvé for a project in Conakry (Guinea).

Page de gauche : L'immeuble des Jousse vu depuis l'autre côté du port de l'Arsenal.
En haut : Sur la terrasse sur le toit, les Jousse ont placé un tabouret rouge et un brise-soleil en aluminium conçu par Prouvé pour un immeuble à Conakry en Guinée.

Gegenüberliegende Seite: Ein Blick auf das Wohnhaus vom Port de l'Arsenal aus.
Oben: Die Dachterrasse haben die Jousses mit einem roten Hocker sowie einer Aluminium-Sonnenblende aus Conakry, Guinea, von Prouvé bestückt.

Clémence and Didier Krzentowski are the owners of Paris's hippest design gallery, Kreo, where they represent the likes of the Bouroullec brothers, Martin Szekely and Marc Newson. They are also avid collectors. As Didier says, "When you collect, the goal is to have the best collection in the world." He believes he has the largest number of lights by designer Gino Sarfatti, and has two other principal passions – Pierre Paulin and mirrors created by artists. Their apartment is certainly jam-packed with an anarchic mix of objects. Among them, several artistic installations, the most striking of which is Richard Jackson's "Accidents in Abstract Painting". Created in situ, it consists of a large model airplane on a paint-spattered sheet. "When he switched on the propellor," recalls Krzentowski enthusiastically, "paint went absolutely everywhere!"

Clémence & Didier Krzentowski

Clémence et Didier Krzentowski sont les propriétaires de la galerie de design super branché Kreo où ils représentent, entre autres, les frères Bouroullec, Martin Szekely et Marc Newson. Ce sont aussi d'avides collectionneurs. Il croit posséder le plus grand nombre de luminaires de Gino Sarfatti et a deux autres grandes passions : Pierre Paulin et les miroirs d'artistes. Leur appartement est bondé d'un mélange anarchique d'objets. Parmi eux, plusieurs installations artistiques dont la plus frappante est « Accidents in Abstract Painting » de Richard Jackson. Créée in situ, c'est une grande maquette d'avion sur un drap éclaboussé de peinture. « Quand il a mis l'hélice en route », se souvient Didier, « il y a eu de la peinture partout ! ».

Clémence und Didier Krzentowski sind die Besitzer von Kreo, der wichtigsten Designgalerie von Paris. Dort vertreten sie unter anderen die Bouroullec-Brüder, Martin Szekely und Marc Newson. Außerdem sind sie begeisterte Sammler. »Wenn man sammelt, besteht das Ziel darin, die beste Sammlung der Welt zu haben«, so Didier. Nach eigener Auskunft besitzt er die größte Anzahl an Lampen des Designers Gino Sarfatti. Er hat aber auch noch zwei andere große Leidenschaften, nämlich für Pierre Paulin und für von Künstlern geschaffene Spiegel. Die Wohnung des Paars ist voll bis unter die Decke mit einem anarchischen Mix verschiedener Objekte. Dazu zählen verschiedene Künstlerinstallationen, von denen Richard Jacksons »Accidents in Abstract Painting« sicherlich die Auffälligste ist. Sie entstand direkt vor Ort und besteht aus einem großen Modellflugzeug, das auf einem farbbespritzten Laken steht. »Als er den Propeller anmachte«, erinnert sich Krzentowski mit Begeisterung, »spritzte die Farbe absolut überall hin!«

Previous pages: The Eiffel Tower is reflected in a stainless-steel and lacquer coffee table by Martin Szekely. The living room is dominated by the Richard Jackson installation "Accidents in Abstract Painting", which features a large model airplane.
Above and right: A red bench by the Bouroullecs and a yellow Pierre Paulin chair are grouped around the Szekely coffee table. The "U.S. Historians" artwork is by Sam Durant.

Pages précédentes : La tour Eiffel se reflète dans une table basse en acier inoxydable et laque de Martin Szekely. Le séjour est dominé par la grande maquette d'avion de l'installation de Richard Jackson, « Accidents in Abstract Painting ».
En haut et à droite : Autour de la table basse de Szekely, un banc rouge des Bouroullec et un siège jaune de Pierre Paulin. Au mur, une œuvre de Sam Durant, « U. S. Historians ».

Vorhergehende Seiten: Der Eiffelturm spiegelt sich in einem Couchtisch aus Edelstahl und Lack von Martin Szekely. Das Wohnzimmer wird von Richard Jacksons Installation »Accidents in Abstract Painting« beherrscht, zu der ein riesiges Modellflugzeug gehört.
Oben und rechts: Eine rote Bank von den Bouroullec-Brüdern und ein gelber Stuhl von Pierre Paulin stehen um den Couchtisch von Szekely. Das Bild mit dem Titel »U.S. Historians« stammt von Sam Durant.

Right: Richard Jackson's plane seems to hover over a Marc Newson coffee table.
Below: Vases by Hella Jongerius, the Bouroullecs and Jerszy Seymour are arranged on top of a Maarten van Severen sideboard. The middle ceiling light is by Gino Sarfatti.

À droite : L'avion de Richard Jackson semble planer au-dessus d'une table basse de Marc Newson.
En bas : Des vases d'Hella Jongerius, des Bouroullec et de Jerszy Seymour sont regroupés sur une desserte de Maarten van Severen. Au centre, un lustre de Gino Sarfatti.

Rechts: Richard Jacksons Flugzeug scheint über dem Couchtisch von Marc Newson zu schweben.
Unten: Vasen von Hella Jongerius, den Bouroullec-Brüdern und Jerszy Seymour wurden auf einem Sideboard von Maarten van Severen arrangiert. Die mittlere Deckenleuchte ist von Gino Sarfatti.

Above: In the dining room is a Szekely table, a Raymond Loewy sideboard, metallic vases by Andrea Branzi, Pierre Paulin wall lights and a Barbara Kruger photomontage.
Right: Vases by Ettore Sottsass, Wieki Somers and Hella Jongerius are displayed on a Martin Szekely bookshelf.
Facing page: The master bedroom features globes by Ange Leccia and an array of coloured rectangles by Allan McCollum.
Following pages: Bookshelves by Alessandro Mendini and Martin Szekely. The boat-like bathtub was created by Wieki Somers.

En haut : Dans la salle à manger, une table de Szekely, un buffet de Raymond Loewy, des vases en métal d'Andrea Branzi, des appliques de Pierre Paulin et un photomontage de Barbara Kruger.
À droite : Des vases d'Ettore Sottsass, de Wieki Somers et d'Hella Jongerius exposés dans une bibliothèque de Martin Szekely.
Page de droite : Dans la chambre de maître, des globes d'Ange Leccia et un arrangement de rectangles de couleurs d'Allan McCollum.
Pages suivantes : Étagères d'Alessandro Mendini et de Martin Szekely. La baignoire bateau a été dessinée par Wieki Somers.

Oben: Im Esszimmer finden sich ein Tisch von Szekely, ein Sideboard von Raymond Loewy, Metallvasen von Andrea Branzi, Wandleuchten von Pierre Paulin und eine Fotoarbeit von Barbara Kruger.
Rechts: Vasen von Ettore Sottsass, Wieki Somers und Hella Jongerius schmücken ein Regal von Martin Szekely.
Gegenüberliegende Seite: Das große Schlafzimmer stellt Globen von Ange Leccia sowie viele bunte Rechtecke von Allan McCollum zur Schau.
Folgende Seiten: Bücherregale von Alessandro Mendini und Martin Szekely. Die Badewanne in Bootsform stammt von Wieki Somers.

Built on the quarries of Montmartre c. 1890, the Cité des Fusains has had many illustrious inhabitants. Artists Pierre Bonnard, Joan Miró and Jean Arp all had studios in the maze-like complex. Since 1993, designer Hubert Le Gall has both lived and worked there. Ask him why and he talks about the "tranquillity". "You really feel like you're in the countryside," he remarks. His house is filled with his own creations. In the entrance hall, a crocodile looks as if it is biting into a mirrored wall light. In the sitting room upstairs are a chair in the form of a whale and Le Gall's famous "Marguerites" table, composed of a bunch of bronze daisies. Throughout, he was keen to maintain the ambience of an "atelier d'artiste". "I wanted to blend in with the space," he explains. In the kitchen, he even hung drawings by one of its former inhabitants, artist René Collamarini.

Hubert Le Gall

Construite sur les carrières de Montmartre vers 1890, la Cité des Fusains a connu de nombreux illustres habitants : Pierre Bonnard, Joan Miró et Jean Arp ont eu leur atelier dans le dédale de ses allées. Depuis 1993, le designer Hubert Le Gall y vit et travaille. Il apprécie sa tranquillité et remarque : « Ici, on a vraiment l'impression d'être à la campagne. » Sa maison est remplie de ses créations. Dans l'entrée, un crocodile semble mordre une applique en miroirs. Le salon à l'étage accueille un fauteuil en forme de baleine et la célèbre table « Marguerites » de Le Gall, composée de fleurs en bronze. Il s'est efforcé de préserver partout l'atmosphère d'un atelier d'artiste. « Je voulais me fondre dans l'espace », explique-t-il. Dans la cuisine, il a même accroché des dessins d'un ancien occupant des lieux, l'artiste René Collamarini.

Die um 1890 auf dem Steinbruch vom Montmartre erbaute Cité des Fusains hatte bereits viele illustre Bewohner. Künstler wie Pierre Bonnard, Joan Miró und Jean Arp besaßen alle Ateliers in dem labyrinthartigen Viertel. Seit 1993 lebt und arbeitet hier auch der Designer Hubert Le Gall. Wenn man ihn nach dem Grund dafür fragt, spricht er von der »Beschaulichkeit und Ruhe«. »Man fühlt sich wirklich wie auf dem Land«, meint er. Sein Haus ist angefüllt mit eigenen Objekten. Im Flur scheint ein Krokodil in eine Wandleuchte mit Spiegeln zu beißen. Im Wohnzimmer im ersten Obergeschoss stehen ein Sessel in Form eines Wals sowie Le Galls berühmter Tisch namens »Marguerites«, der aus einem Strauß bronzener Margeriten besteht. Er hat durchgängig darauf geachtet, dass die Atmosphäre eines »atelier d'artiste« erhalten bleibt. »Ich wollte mich an den Raum anpassen«, erklärt er. In der Küche hat er sogar Zeichnungen von einem vorherigen Bewohner, dem Künstler René Collamarini, aufgehängt.

Previous pages: A bust by René Collamarini stands in the bucolic courtyard in front of Le Gall's house.
Right: One of Le Gall's "Trèfle" (Clover) chairs can be seen in front of an original, plaster relief fireplace, which he also designed. The candles actually light up and the hands of the clock turn.
Below: A crocodile bites into a mirrored wall light in the entrance hall. The 19th-century cartonnier was originally devised for storing drawings.

Pages précédentes : Un buste de René Collamarini dans la cour bucolique devant la maison de Le Gall.
À droite : Une des chaises « Trèfle » de Le Gall devant une fausse cheminée en plâtre, également dessinée par le maître de maison. Les bougies s'allument vraiment et les aiguilles de la pendule tournent.
En bas : Un crocodile mord une applique à deux miroirs dans l'entrée. Le cartonnier du XIXᵉ siècle fut conçu à l'origine pour ranger des dessins.

Vorhergehende Seiten: Eine Büste von René Collamarini steht im idyllischen Hof vor Le Galls Haus.
Rechts: Einer von Le Galls »Trèfle« (Klee)-Stühlen ist vor einem Gipsrelief in Form eines Kamins zu sehen, das er ebenfalls entwarf. Die Kerzen lassen sich tatsächlich anzünden, und die Zeiger der Uhr bewegen sich.
Unten: Im Flur beißt ein Krokodil in eine Wandleuchte mit Spiegeln. Der Cartonnier aus dem 19. Jahrhundert diente ursprünglich der Aufbewahrung von Zeichnungen.

Above: The "Pot de Fleur" (Flower Pot) sofa, "Sunset" bookshelves and "Marguerites" coffee tables were all designed by Le Gall.
Right: A bronze chest called "Taureau" (Bull) stands at the bottom of the stairs.
Following pages: Most of the objects in the living room were created by Le Gall, among them the "Whale" chair, the "Mulus" mirror and the green lacquer and gilt bronze "Pré Emballé" chest. Touches of wit abound. His "vice versa" vases can be displayed both ways up and the chimney surround in the sitting room doubles as a blackboard.

En haut : Le canapé « Pot de fleur », la bibliothèque « Sunset » et les tables basses « Marguerites » sont tous des créations de Le Gall.
À droite : Au pied de l'escalier, un coffre en bronze baptisé « Taureau ».
Pages suivantes : La plupart des objets du séjour ont été créés par Le Gall, comme le fauteuil « Whale », le miroir « Mulus » et le coffre en bronze doré et laque verte « Pré Emballé ». Les touches d'humour sont partout : ses vases « vice versa » peuvent être posés dans un sens ou dans l'autre. Le cadre de cheminée fait aussi office de tableau noir.

Oben: Das »Pot de Fleur«-Sofa, die »Sunset«-Regale und der »Marguerites«-Couchtisch sind alles Entwürfe von Le Gall.
Rechts: Am Fuß der Treppe steht die Bronzekommode »Taureau« (Stier).
Folgende Seiten: Die meisten Objekte im Wohnzimmer wurden von Le Gall selbst entworfen. Dazu zählen auch der »Wal«-Sessel, die sogenannten »Mulus«-Spiegel und die Kommode »Pré Emballé« aus grünem Lack und vergoldeter Bronze. Nichts ist hier ohne Hintersinn: Seine »vice versa«-Vasen können von beiden Seiten benutzt werden, und die Kamineinfassung dient gleichzeitig als Tafel.

Nathalie Lété and Thomas Fougeirol have found the perfect way to combine professional and family life. They are both artists. Thomas is a painter and Nathalie creates a whole array of things, from earthenware for Astier de Villatte to children's clothes for the Japanese label Muchacha. They live in a loft-like space in what was once a metal factory in Ivry-sur-Seine. In the same complex, each also has a studio… which means that they are never far from their two children, Angèle and Oskar. Thomas's main brief for the two-storey flat was that there be lots of storage space. "He didn't want there to be any room for paintings because he knew that I'd take over every wall," laughs Lété. Undaunted, she filled the place with other creations instead: carpets, cushions and ceramics, which evoke a world of insects, flowers and East European folk art.

Nathalie Lété & Thomas Fougeirol

Les artistes Nathalie Lété et Thomas Fougeirol ont trouvé la solution idéale pour conjuguer vie professionnelle et vie privée. Thomas est peintre et Nathalie crée toutes sortes de choses, de la faïence pour Astier de Villatte à des vêtements d'enfants pour la marque japonaise Muchacha. Leur appartement/loft est situé dans une ancienne usine de métaux à Ivry-sur-Seine. Thomas tenait à ce que l'espace de deux étages comporte beaucoup de rangements. « Il ne voulait pas de tableaux, sachant qu'ils envahiraient rapidement tous les murs », se souvient Nathalie en riant. Du coup, elle a rempli l'espace avec d'autres créations : tapis, coussins, artisanat d'Europe de l'Est et céramiques évoquant un monde d'insectes et de fleurs.

Nathalie Lété und Thomas Fougeirol haben es geschafft, Beruf und Familie perfekt miteinander zu vereinen. Beide sind Künstler: Thomas ist Maler, und Nathalie entwirft alles Mögliche, von Keramik für Astier de Villatte bis hin zu Kinderkleidung für das japanische Label Muchacha. Sie wohnen in einer Art Loft in Ivry-sur-Seine, das einmal eine Metallfabrik war. Im selben Gebäude hat jeder noch sein eigenes Atelier. So sind sie immer in der Nähe ihrer beiden Kinder Angèle und Oskar. Thomas kam es vor allem darauf an, dass die über zwei Geschosse gehende Wohnung genügend Stauraum hat. »Er wollte, dass nirgendwo mehr Platz für meine Bilder ist, weil ich sonst jede Wand zugepflastert hätte«, sagt Lété lachend. Dafür füllte sie den noch verbliebenen Raum todesmutig mit ihren anderen Kreationen wie Teppichen, Kissen und Keramik. Sie beschwören eine Welt voller Insekten, Blumen und osteuropäischer Volkskunst.

Previous pages: In Lété's atelier are several cardboard bas-reliefs, which she created in tandem with Mathias Robert under the name "Mathias et Nathalie". They hang above a chest, which comes from a French electricity board factory.
Above: In the master bedroom is a painted chest from Pakistan. The iron ladder leads up to the bedroom of the couple's daughter, Angèle.
Right: On the first-floor landing is an oil painting by Fougeirol. The armchair used to belong to his grandmother.

Pages précédentes : Dans l'atelier de Lété, des bas-relief en carton, créés par Lété avec Mathias Robert sous le nom « Mathias et Nathalie », sont accrochés au-dessus d'un coffre provenant d'une centrale électrique.
En haut : Dans la chambre principale, une armoire peinte du Pakistan. L'échelle métallique mène à la chambre d'Angèle, la fille du couple.
À droite : Sur le palier du premier étage, une huile de Fougeirol. Le fauteuil appartenait à sa grand-mère.

Vorhergehende Seiten: In Létés Atelier finden sich mehrere Pappreliefs, die sie gemeinsam mit Mathias Robert unter dem Namen »Mathias et Nathalie« entwarf. Sie hängen über einem Schrank, der aus einem französischen Elektrizitätswerk stammt.
Oben: Im Schlafzimmer steht ein bemalter Schrank aus Pakistan. Die Eisenleiter führt in das Zimmer der Tochter Angèle.
Rechts: Im Flur im oberen Geschoss hängt ein Ölgemälde von Fougeirol. Der Sessel gehörte einst seiner Großmutter.

New Paris Interiors   Nathalie Lété & Thomas Fougeirol

Right: Lété created the carpets and garland in Angèle's room. The contemporary cotton bedspread is from Greece.
Below: In the living room, the oak coffee table was specially created by Antonis Cardew. The sofa is from the Parisian store Caravane. The yellow lamp is made from sections of water pipes.
Following pages: Lété's own creations are omnipresent throughout both her home and atelier. They include hand-painted plates and ceramic objects inspired by marine life. The vase on the dining table is from Cliousclat in Provence and the glasses from Biot.

À droite : Lété a créé les tapis et la guirlande de la chambre d'Angèle. Le couvre-lit moderne en coton vient de Grèce.
Ci-dessous : Dans le séjour, la table basse en chêne a été créée spécialement par Antonis Cardew.
Pages suivantes : Les créations de Lété sont omniprésentes dans l'appartement et l'atelier ; parmi elles, des assiettes et des objets en céramique d'inspiration marine peints à la main. La cruche sur la table vient de la fabrique provençale de Cliousclat et les verres de la maison Biot.

Rechts: Lété schuf die Teppiche und Girlanden in Angèles Zimmer. Der Bettüberwurf stammt aus Griechenland.
Unten: Der Eichencouchtisch ist eine Sonderanfertigung von Antonis Cardew. Das Sofa stammt aus dem Pariser Einrichtungshaus »Caravane«. Die gelbe Lampe besteht aus zusammengesetzten Wasserrohren.
Folgende Seiten: Létés eigene Kreationen sind in der Wohnung und ihrem Atelier überall präsent. Dazu gehören auch handbemalte Teller und Keramikobjekte, die von Meereslebewesen inspiriert sind. Die Vase auf dem Esstisch ist aus Cliousclat in der Provence, und die Gläser stammen aus Biot.

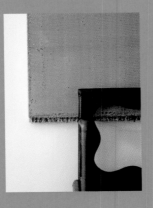

Christian Liaigre is one of France's most lauded living designers. Among his most celebrated projects to date are The Mercer Hotel in New York and apartments for Calvin Klein and Rupert Murdoch. When it comes to his own flat in Paris, he claims not to make that much effort. If that is the case, then it certainly doesn't show! The eight-room duplex in the Marais district was formerly home to a clothing factory. Liaigre ripped everything out and created a wonderfully elegant shell for his ever-changing pieces of furniture. "As it's my profession, I quickly get sick of things," he admits. What remains, however, are his works of art and the objects he brings back from his travels. They include a Buddha head, which he found in Thailand 25 years ago, and sculpted coconut shells from Saint Barths.

Christian Liaigre

Christian Liaigre est un des décorateurs vivants les plus admirés de France. Ses réalisations célèbres incluent l'hôtel Mercer à New York et les appartements de Calvin Klein et de Rupert Murdoch. Pour sa propre résidence à Paris, il affirme ne pas s'être donné beaucoup de mal. À la voir, on ne le dirait pas ! Son duplex de 8 pièces dans le Marais était autrefois une usine de confection. Il a abattu tous les murs et créé un élégant écrin pour son mobilier en évolution constante. « Comme c'est mon métier, je me lasse vite », avoue-t-il. En revanche, il tient à ses œuvres d'art et aux objets qu'il rapporte de ses voyages. Parmi eux, une tête de bouddha trouvée en Thaïlande il y a 25 ans et des noix de coco sculptées venant de Saint Barths.

Christian Liaigre ist einer von Frankreichs meistgepriesenen zeitgenössischen Designern. Zu seinen berühmtesten Projekten zählen bislang das Mercer Hotel in New York sowie Wohnungen für Calvin Klein und Rupert Murdoch. Bei seinem eigenen Appartement in Paris habe er sich nicht so angestrengt, behauptet er. Davon ist allerdings nichts zu merken! In dem Acht-Zimmer-Domizil im Marais war einst eine Kleiderfabrik untergebracht. Liaigre riss alles raus und schuf eine wunderbar elegante Hülle für seine sich stets ändernde Einrichtung. »Ich bekomme die Dinge sehr schnell satt, eine Art Berufskrankheit«, gibt er zu. Was bleibt, sind seine Kunstwerke und Reisesouvenirs. Dazu gehören der Kopf eines Buddhas, den er vor 25 Jahren in Thailand fand, sowie mit Schnitzereien verzierte Kokosnussschalen aus Saint Barths.

Facing page: Both the chestnut stools and iron kitchen table were created by Liaigre.
Following pages: Numerous Liaigre designs can be found in the sitting room. Among them are the "Galet" coffee table, the "Bazane" stool and the "Latin" chair. The photograph is by Peter Beard. Among the historical objects in the flat are an 18th-century Swedish sofa and a Buddha's head, which Liaigre found in Thailand.

Page de droite : Les tabourets en châtaignier et la table en fer sont des créations de Liaigre.
Pages suivantes : Dans le séjour, de nombreuses créations de Liaigre, dont une table basse « Galet », un tabouret « Bazane » et une chaise « Latin ». Les photos sont de Peter Beard. L'appartement contient également des objets anciens comme un sofa suédois du XVIIIᵉ siècle et une tête de bouddha que Liaigre a rapportée de Thaïlande.

Gegenüberliegende Seite: Sowohl die Hocker aus Kastanienholz als auch der eiserne Küchentisch sind Entwürfe von Liaigre.
Folgende Seiten: Verschiedene Liaigre-Entwürfe finden sich auch im Wohnzimmer. Dazu zählen der Couchtisch »Galet«, der Hocker »Bazane« und der sogenannte »Latin«-Stuhl. Die Fotoarbeit ist von Peter Beard. Zu den antiken Gegenständen in der Wohnung gehören ein schwedisches Sofa aus dem 18. Jahrhundert sowie ein Buddhakopf, den Liaigre in Thailand aufgetrieben hat.

Previous pages: In the sitting room, a Chinese table stands in front of a picture of a colocynth by Jacques Martinez. The paper frieze is by the same artist.
Above: The office is decorated with African stools and wickerwork. The blinds are made from linen.
Right: The 120-square-metre garden can be seen behind a copy of a Greek head.

Pages précédentes : Dans le séjour, une table chinoise devant un tableau représentant une coloquinte de Jacques Martinez. La frise en papier est du même artiste.
En haut : Le bureau est décoré avec des tabourets et de la vannerie africains. Les stores sont en lin.
À droite : On aperçoit le jardin de 120 mètres carrés derrière une copie d'une tête grecque.

Vorhergehende Seiten: Im Wohnzimmer steht ein chinesischer Tisch vor dem Bild einer Koloquinte von Jacques Martinez. Der Papierfries stammt vom selben Künstler.
Oben: Das Büro schmücken afrikanische Hocker und Körbe. Die Rollos sind aus Leinen.
Rechts: Hinter der Kopie eines griechischen Porträts erhascht man einen Blick auf den 120 Quadratmeter großen Garten.

"It's difficult for me to travel somewhere and not come back with something," admits the world-famous shoe designer Christian Louboutin. His Parisian apartment is filled with many of his finds – a vase from Peru, a lamp from Beirut, a portrait of an Indian woman from Jodhpur, a Hungarian cavalier's belt from Vienna... The actual flat is situated in the area known as the "Nouvelle Athènes", just a stone's throw away from the sex shops of Pigalle. When it comes to interiors, Louboutin hates corridors and can't abide skylights. "They make me feel like I'm an orchid in a greenhouse," he quips. He does, on the other hand, love theatrical décors. Rather fittingly, the imposing, silvered chest in the dining room was originally a stage prop for a production of "The Merchant of Venice"!

Christian Louboutin

« Chaque fois que je voyage, j'ai du mal à ne pas rapporter quelque chose », avoue Christian Louboutin, créateur de chaussures mondialement connu. Son appartement parisien, situé dans la Nouvelle Athènes à deux pas des sex-shops de Pigalle, est rempli de ses trouvailles : un vase péruvien, une lampe de Beyrouth, un portrait d'Indienne de Jodhpur, une ceinture de cavalier hongrois dénichée à Vienne... En matière d'architecture intérieure, il déteste les couloirs et les lucarnes. « Elles me donnent l'impression d'être une orchidée en serre. » En revanche, il adore les ambiances théâtrales. D'ailleurs, l'imposant coffre argenté de sa salle à manger faisait autrefois partie d'un décor pour « Le Marchand de Venise »!

»Es fällt mir schwer, irgendwohin zu reisen und nichts mitzubringen«, gibt der weltberühmte Schuhdesigner Christian Louboutin zu. Seine Pariser Wohnung ist mit zahlreichen Fundstücken angefüllt – dazu zählen eine Vase aus Peru, eine Lampe aus Beirut, das Porträt einer Inderin aus Jodhpur, der Gürtel eines ungarischen Reiters aus Wien ... Die Wohnung liegt in dem Viertel, das als »Nouvelle Athènes« bezeichnet wird, nur ein Steinwurf von den Sexshops um die Place Pigalle entfernt. Wenn es um die Inneneinrichtung geht, hasst Louboutin Flure und kann auch Oberlichter nicht ausstehen. »Bei ihnen fühle ich mich wie eine Orchidee im Gewächshaus«, witzelt er. Dafür liebt er theatralisches Dekor. Passenderweise war der eindrucksvolle, versilberte Schrank im Esszimmer ursprünglich eine Bühnendekoration für eine Produktion von »Der Kaufmann von Venedig«!

Above: *In the sitting room, a chair that Napoleon gave to one of his generals stands to the left of the fireplace. To the right, a beaded Senegalese armchair, which Louboutin found in New York.*
Right: *A Garouste & Bonetti cabinet made from bronze and clay.*

En haut : *Dans le salon, à gauche de la cheminée, une chaise offerte par Napoléon à un de ses généraux. À droite, un fauteuil sénégalais en perles, acheté par Louboutin à New York.*
À droite : *Un cabinet en bronze et argile de Garouste & Bonetti.*

Oben: *Im Wohnzimmer steht links vom Kamin ein Stuhl, den Napoleon einem seiner Generäle schenkte. Rechts befindet sich ein perlenbestickter Sessel aus dem Senegal, den Louboutin in New York entdeckt hat.*
Rechts: *Ein Schrank von Garouste & Bonetti aus Bronze und Ton.*

Above: The dining room chairs are by Charlotte Perriand. The silvered chest was originally made for a stage production of "The Merchant of Venice."
Right: On the dining table, earthenware from the Atelier Jean Faucon d'Apt.

En haut : Les chaises de la salle à manger sont de Charlotte Perriand. Le coffre argenté fut conçu pour une production du « Marchand de Venise ».
À droite : Sur la table de la salle à manger, de la vaisselle en faïence d'Apt de l'atelier de Jean Faucon.

Oben: Die Esszimmerstühle sind von Charlotte Perriand. Der versilberte Schrank wurde ursprünglich für eine Theaterproduktion von »Der Kaufmann von Venedig« angefertigt.
Rechts: Auf dem Esstisch steht Steingutgeschirr aus dem Atelier Jean Faucon in Apt.

Right: A lamp from Beirut, a drawing by Gérard Garouste, a Hungarian cavalier's belt and a François Morellet metallic sculpture sit on top of a 1930s neo-colonial sideboard in the dining room.
Below: In the sitting room, a 1940s sofa and an armchair stand on a Bedouin rug from Mauritania. The parchment-clad chest was designed by André Arbus and the top of the 1930s American coffee table is made from Bakelite.

À droite : Dans la salle à manger, une lampe rapportée de Beyrouth, un dessin de Gérard Garouste, une ceinture de cavalier hongrois et une sculpture en métal de François Morellet sur une console néocoloniale des années 1930.
En bas : Dans le salon, un canapé et un fauteuil des années 1940 sur un tapis bédouin provenant de Mauritanie. Le coffre tapissé de parchemin a été dessiné par André Arbus. Le plateau de la table basse américaine des années 1930 est en bakélite.

Rechts: Eine Lampe aus Beirut, eine Zeichnung von Gérard Garouste, der Gürtel eines ungarischen Reiters und eine Metallskulptur von François Morellet befinden sich auf dem Sideboard aus den 1930er-Jahren im Neokolonialstil.
Unten: Im Wohnzimmer stehen ein Sofa und ein Sessel aus den 1940er-Jahren auf einem Beduinenteppich aus Mauretanien. Der pergamentbespannte Schrank ist ein Entwurf von André Arbus, und die Tischplatte des amerikanischen Couchtischs aus den 1930er-Jahren ist aus Bakelit.

Architect India Mahdavi's flat has many things going for it. It is situated in the Hôtel d'Artagnan, once home to the famous musketeer. It comes with a garage (a rarity in Paris) and is right by her office, from where she has overseen projects like the Townhouse hotel in Miami and the Dragon-i restaurant in Hong Kong. Inside, it boasts a number of interesting quirks. Versailles-style parquet is juxtaposed with oversized 1930s mouldings and the overall layout is an unusual L-shape. The heart of the apartment is the dining room, for which Mahdavi created a custom corner banquette. "It's used as a family room," she declares. "We have drinks there. My son does his homework there." The flat's biggest asset, however, is outside – the view over the Paul Claudel gardens. "Every day," she says, "I look out and say how lucky I am!"

India Mahdavi

L'appartement de l'architecte India Mahdavi présente de nombreux avantages : il possède un garage (une rareté à Paris) et se trouve à deux pas de son bureau où elle a supervisé des projets tels que l'hôtel Townhouse à Miami ou le restaurant Dragon-i à Hong Kong. En forme de L, il est situé dans l'Hôtel d'Artagnan où a vécu le célèbre mousquetaire et qui comporte des excentricités intéressantes, comme la juxtaposition d'un parquet Versailles et de moulures surdimensionnées des années 1930. La salle à manger, pour laquelle Mahdavi a créé une banquette en coin, est le cœur du foyer. « On s'en sert comme d'un séjour », explique-t-elle. « On y prend l'apéro, mon fils y fait ses devoirs. » Toutefois, son plus grand atout, c'est la vue sur les jardins Paul Claudel. « Tous les jours, je regarde par la fenêtre et me dis que j'ai de la chance. »

Die Wohnung der Architektin India Mahdavi hat viele Vorzüge. Sie befindet sich im Hôtel d'Artagnan, in dem einst der berühmte Musketier lebte. Eine Garage gehört auch dazu (was in Paris eine Seltenheit ist). Außerdem liegt die Wohnung direkt neben ihrem Büro, von dem aus sie Projekte wie das Townhouse Hotel in Miami und das Dragon-i-Restaurant in Hongkong überwacht. In ihrem Appartement hält sie zahlreiche Überraschungen bereit. Das Parkett im Versailles-Stil wird von riesigen Zierleisten aus den 1930er-Jahren konterkariert. Der Grundriss folgt einer ungewöhnlichen L-Form. Das Herz der Wohnung ist das Esszimmer, für das Mahdavi eine Eckbank entwarf. »Es dient als Familienzimmer«, sagt sie. »Hier nehmen wir unsere Drinks, und mein Sohn macht Hausaufgaben.« Der größte Pluspunkt der Wohnung ist jedoch der Blick auf den Paul-Claudel-Park. »Ich sehe aus dem Fenster und denke mir jeden Tag, was für ein riesiges Glück ich habe!«

© Philippe Chancel

Left: More Mahdavi creations in the living room. The bench is made from sapelli wood and the "Lollipop" lamp from chrome.
Below: For the dining room, Mahdavi created an L-shaped banquette. The photo on the left is by Paolo Nozolino. The candleholder is from Mexico.

À gauche : D'autres créations de Mahdavi dans le salon. Le banc est en sapelli et le lampadaire en chrome.
En bas : Madhavi a dessiné cette banquette en L pour sa salle à manger. La photo sur la gauche est de Paolo Nozolino. Le bougeoir est mexicain.

Links: Im Wohnzimmer gibt es noch mehr Mahdavi-Design. Die Bank ist aus Sapelliholz und die »Lollipop«-Lampe aus Chrom.
Unten: Für das Esszimmer entwarf Mahdavi eine L-förmige Bank. Das Foto links ist von Paolo Nozolino. Der Kerzenständer stammt aus Mexiko.

Previous pages: In the living room, a Flos lamp stands on top of a formica and walnut desk designed by Pierre Paulin. The 1940s Plexiglas chair was bought from the Chahan Gallery.
Facing page: India Mahdavi designed both the chairs, upholstered in Tibetan lambskin, and the iroko wood "Bishop" occasional table. The lamp was a flea-market find.

Pages précédentes : Dans le séjour, une lampe Flos sur un bureau en noyer et formica de Pierre Paulin. La chaise en Plexiglas des années 1940 a été achetée à la galerie Chahan.
Page de gauche : Mahdavi a dessiné les chaises tapissées de peau d'agneau tibétain et la table d'appoint « Bishop » en iroko. La lampe a été chinée aux Puces.

Vorhergehende Seiten: Im Wohnzimmer steht eine Lampe von Flos auf einem Schreibtisch aus Formica und Walnussholz von Pierre Paulin. Der Plexiglas-Stuhl aus den 1940er-Jahren wurde in der Galerie Chahan erworben.
Gegenüberliegende Seite: India Mahdavi entwarf beide Stühle, die mit tibetischem Lammfell bezogen sind, und den Beistelltisch »Bishop« aus Irokoholz. Die Lampe ist ein Fundstück vom Flohmarkt.

Above: The two sofas are Mahdavi prototypes upholstered in velvet. Her "Butterfly" coffee table is made from walnut.
Right: An Arne Jacobsen chair stands in one corner of the master bedroom. The "Swing Still" standing light was designed by Mahdavi.
Facing page: A Jean Prouvé daybed sits in front of a photo of the room taken by Derek Hudson. The standing lamp is from Editions Florence Lopez.

En haut : Les deux canapés tapissés en velours sont des prototypes de Mahdavi. Sa table basse « Butterfly » est en noyer.
À droite : Une chaise d'Arne Jacobsen dans un coin de la chambre principale. Le lampadaire dessiné par Madhavi est baptisé « Swing Still ».
Page de droite : Un lit de repos de Jean Prouvé devant une photo de la pièce prise par Derek Hudson. Le lampadaire vient des Editions Florence Lopez.

Oben: Die beiden Sofas sind mit Samt bezogene Mahdavi-Prototypen. Ihr »Butterfly«-Couchtisch ist aus Walnussholz.
Rechts: Ein Stuhl von Arne Jacobsen steht in einer Ecke des Schlafzimmers. Die von Mahdavi entworfene Stehlampe heißt »Swing Still«.
Gegenüberliegende Seite: Eine Jean-Prouvé-Liege steht vor einer Fotografie des Zimmers von Derek Hudson. Die Stehlampe ist von Editions Florence Lopez.

Perched nine floors up on the top of a building on the Right Bank, Sean McEvoy's flat affords spectacular vistas of the cityscape. The bedroom looks out onto Sacré-Cœur and the Eiffel Tower, the sitting room onto the famous Parisian rooftops. When the American architect first saw the space, it was very different – "a series of small rooms with a rusting veranda at the front". As there were no supporting walls, he was able to rip everything out and start all over again. The result is both free-flowing and refreshingly open. The cube, which contains the bathroom and closets, does not touch the ceiling. The kitchen is defined simply by a five-metre-long Corian bar and there are no curtains or blinds on the windows. The decoration is also deliberately simple. "What's important here is Paris," states McEvoy. "I didn't want anything to compete with that view."

Sean McEvoy

Situé au neuvième et dernier étage d'un immeuble de la rive droite, l'appartement de l'architecte américain Sean McEvoy jouit de vues spectaculaires. La chambre donne sur le Sacré-Cœur et la tour Eiffel, le salon sur les célèbres toits de Paris. Quand il l'a vu la première fois, il n'y avait « qu'une série de petites pièces avec une véranda rouillée sur le devant ». Comme il n'y avait pas de murs porteurs, il a pu tout abattre et repartir de rien. Le résultat est fluide, ouvert et frais. Le cube qui contient la salle de bains et des placards ne touche pas le plafond. La cuisine est définie simplement par un bar en Corian de cinq mètres de long. Il n'y a ni rideaux ni stores aux fenêtres. La décoration est délibérément dépouillée. « L'important ici, c'est Paris », explique-t-il. « Je ne voulais rien qui puisse détourner l'attention de cette vue. »

Das Appartement von Sean McEvoy schwebt in der neunten Etage über dem Dach eines Hauses am rechten Seine-Ufer und bietet einen spektakulären Ausblick auf die Stadt. Vom Schlafzimmer schaut man auf die Kirche Sacré-Cœur und den Eiffelturm, vom Wohnzimmer über die berühmten Pariser Dächer. Als der amerikanische Architekt das erste Mal in der Wohnung stand, sah sie ganz anders aus – »mehrere kleine Zimmer mit einer rostigen Veranda davor«. Da es sich nicht um tragende Wände handelte, konnte er alle rausreißen und ganz von vorn beginnen. Das Ergebnis sind ineinanderfließende, erfrischend offene Räume. Der Kubus, der das Bad und Einbauschränke enthält, berührt die Decke nicht. Die Küche wird einfach nur durch eine fünf Meter lange Theke aus Corian abgetrennt, und die Fenster besitzen weder Vorhänge noch Rollos. Die Einrichtung ist bewusst schlicht gehalten. »Auf Paris kommt es an«, so McEvoy. »Nichts sollte mit dieser Aussicht konkurrieren.«

Previous pages: *Sean McEvoy (in blue) refurbished a glass veranda at the front of the loft-like apartment. The sitting room offers breath-taking views over the rooftops of Paris. The 1950s Pierre Paulin chairs are upholstered in Leatherette and the 1949 Max Bill coffee table is made from birch and linoleum.*
Above: *The kitchen counter is made from Corian.*
Right: *A view from the sitting area into the kitchen. The stools are the "Hi-Pad" model, designed by Jasper Morrison for Cappellini.*
Facing page: *The sofa is a re-edition by Habitat of a Robin Day design.*

Pages précédentes : *Sean McEvoy (en bleu) a retapé la véranda en verre sur le devant de son appartement de style loft. Le séjour offre des vues superbes sur les toits de Paris. Les chaises de Pierre Paulin sont tapissées en skaï et la table basse de Max Bill datée de 1949 est en bois de bouleau et en linoléum.*
En haut : *Le comptoir de la cuisine est en Corian.*
À droite : *Une vue de la cuisine depuis le séjour. Les tabourets « Hi-Pad » ont été dessinés par Jasper Morrison pour Cappellini.*
Page de droite : *Le canapé est une réédition d'un modèle de Robin Day par Habitat.*

Vorhergehende Seiten: *Sean McEvoy (in Blau) ließ die Glasveranda vor der loftartigen Wohnung renovieren. Das Wohnzimmer bietet einen atemberaubenden Blick über die Dächer von Paris. Die Pierre-Paulin-Sessel sind mit Kunstleder bezogen, und der Couchtisch von Max Bill von 1949 besteht aus Birkenholz und Linoleum.*
Oben: *Die Küchentheke ist aus Corian.*
Rechts: *Ein Blick aus dem Wohnzimmerbereich auf die Küche. Die Bar-hocker sind das Modell »Hi-Pad«, von Jasper Morrison für Cappellini.*
Gegenüberliegende Seite: *Das Sofa ist eine Wiederauflage eines Robin-Day-Entwurfs von Habitat.*

New Paris Interiors   Sean McEvoy

Above: Jenny the dog lies in front of a block which houses both the bathroom and closets.
Right: The birch plywood desk was designed by McEvoy. The title of the Wout Berger photo is "Ruigoord II".

En haut : La chienne Jenny est couchée devant le cube qui accueille la salle de bains et des placards.
À droite : Le bureau en contreplaqué de bouleau a été dessiné par McEvoy. La photo de Wout Berger s'intitule « Ruigoord II ».

Oben: Jenny, der Hund, liegt vor einem Kubus, in dem das Bad und Einbauschränke untergebracht sind.
Rechts: Der Sperrholztisch aus Birke wurde von McEvoy entworfen. Das Foto von Wout Berger heißt »Ruigoord II«.

New Paris Interiors   Sean McEvoy

Right: The bedroom looks out onto Sacré-Cœur and the Eiffel Tower.
The wooden vase was made by Jérôme Abel Seguin.
Below: McEvoy created the base of the bed. The 1950s fibre glass and
steel chair was designed by Gabriel Vacher and the articulated lamp
bought at the Montreuil flea market.

À droite : La chambre donne sur le Sacré-Cœur et la tour Eiffel. Le
vase en bois a été réalisé par Jérôme Abel Seguin.
En bas : McEvoy a dessiné la base du lit. La chaise en acier et fibre de
verre est de Gabriel Vacher. La lampe articulée a été trouvée aux
Puces de Montreuil.

Rechts: Vom Schlafzimmer geht der Blick auf die Kirche Sacré-Cœur
und den Eiffelturm. Die Holzvase ist von Jérôme Abel Seguin.
Unten: McEvoy baute das Bettgestell. Der Sessel aus Fiberglas und
Stahl ist ein Entwurf von Gabriel Vacher und die bewegliche Lampe
ein Fund vom Flohmarkt in Montreuil.

In recent times, decorator Frédéric Méchiche has completely changed his modus vivendi. He bought a home in Saint-Tropez and made it his main base. He also acquired a boat called "Hornblower II" and decided to swap his large Parisian apartment for a 50-square-meter pied-à-terre. "I wanted something unusual, with personality," he states. He certainly got that. The flat is situated in an early 1930s building in the Bauhaus style, which used to house a jewellery workshop. Its predominant feature is a huge glass window, which floods it with light. Méchiche completely gutted the inside and decided to open up the space. It took three weeks simply to remove the layers of parquet, carpet and glue to reveal the original concrete floor! He then filled it with original editions of design classics. Among them, a coffee table by Ludwig Mies van der Rohe, several Arne Jacobsen lights and a set of chairs by Charles & Ray Eames.

Frédéric Méchiche

Récemment, le décorateur Frédéric Méchiche a radicalement modifié ses habitudes. Il s'est acheté une maison à Saint-Tropez dont il a fait sa base, un bateau baptisé Hornblower II et a abandonné son grand appartement parisien pour un pied-à-terre de 50 mètres carrés. « Je voulais quelque chose de spécial, qui ait du caractère », explique-t-il. De fait, il n'en manque pas. Il se situe dans un immeuble du début des années 1930 de style Bauhaus qui abritait autrefois un atelier de joaillerie. Pour mettre en valeur l'immense verrière, Méchiche a abattu les murs et ouvert l'espace inondé de lumière. Il a fallu trois semaines rien que pour arracher les couches de parquet, de moquette et de colle pour mettre à nu le sol d'origine en béton. Il l'a ensuite meublé d'éditions originales de classiques du design, dont une table basse de Mies van der Rohe, plusieurs luminaires d'Arne Jacobsen et un ensemble de sièges de Charles & Ray Eames.

Vor Kurzem hat Innenarchitekt Frédéric Méchiche seinen Modus Vivendi radikal geändert. Er kaufte sich ein Haus in St. Tropez und machte es zu seinem Hauptwohnsitz. Außerdem erwarb er ein Boot namens Hornblower II und beschloss, sein großes Pariser Appartement gegen ein 50 Quadratmeter großes Pied-à-terre einzutauschen. »Ich wollte etwas Ungewöhnliches mit Charakter«, so Méchiche. Und genau das hat er gefunden. Die Wohnung befindet sich in einem Gebäude, das Anfang der 1930er-Jahre im Bauhausstil errichtet wurde. Früher war darin eine Goldschmiedewerkstatt untergebracht. Ihr auffälligstes Merkmal ist ein riesiges Glasfenster, sodass sie lichtdurchflutet ist. Méchiche hat die Wohnung komplett entkernt und einen großen Raum geschaffen. Es dauerte allein drei Wochen, die Parkett-, Teppich- und Leimschichten herauszureißen, um den Original-Betonboden freizulegen! Anschließend richtete er die Wohnung mit originalen Designklassikern ein. Dazu zählen ein Couchtisch von Mies van der Rohe, verschiedene Arne-Jacobsen-Lampen und eine Stuhlgruppe von Charles & Ray Eames.

Fashion designer Rick Owens lives and works in a building on Place du Palais Bourbon, originally built as a present from Napoleon to one of his generals. In more recent times, it was also home to the Socialist Party headquarters. Today, his press office is located in the wonderfully elaborate rooms at the front. "I couldn't work in it," asserts Owens, "because it faces the Place and I'd get too distracted." Instead, he has his office at the back in a 1950s annex, which looks out on the gardens of the French Defence Ministry. On the second floor is the fur studio – the domain of his partner, Michèle Lamy, which he calls "Lamy Land". Together, they decided to rip out the former office fittings and leave much of the interior raw. "It would have been a daunting project to clean everything up," he explains, "and we're fine with it just as it is."

Rick Owens & Michèle Lamy

Le designer de mode Rick Owens vit et travaille dans un immeuble de la place du Palais Bourbon qui a servi de Q. G. au parti socialiste. Le service de presse d'Owens est situé dans des pièces superbes donnant sur la façade. « Je ne pouvais pas y travailler, la vue est trop distrayante » confie Owens. Il a installé son propre bureau à l'arrière, dans une annexe des années 1950 avec vue sur les jardins du ministère de la Défense. Le premier étage, « Lamy Land », accueille le département des fourrures, le domaine de son associée Michèle Lamy. Ensemble, ils ont décidé d'arracher l'équipement de bureau et de laisser une grande partie de l'espace brut. « Tout refaire aurait nécessité un travail colossal et l'espace nous convient tel qu'il est », explique-t-il.

Der Modedesigner Rick Owens lebt und arbeitet in einem Gebäude an der Place du Palais Bourbon, das einst ein Geschenk von Napoleon an einen seiner Generäle war. In jüngerer Zeit war hier das Parteibüro der Sozialisten untergebracht. Heute befindet sich Owens PR-Büro in den wunderbar reich verzierten Räumen zur Straße hin. »Ich könnte nicht dort arbeiten«, so Owens, »weil es auf die Place hinausgeht, und das würde mich zu sehr ablenken.« Sein Büro liegt im Anbau aus den 1950er-Jahren, der nach hinten auf die Gärten des französischen Verteidigungsministeriums hinausgeht. Im ersten Obergeschoss befindet sich das Pelzstudio – die Arbeitsdomäne seiner Partnerin Michèle Lamy, die er nur »Lamy Land« nennt. Gemeinsam beschlossen sie, die früheren Büroeinrichtungen herauszureißen und die Räume überwiegend im Rohzustand zu belassen. »Es hätte einen enormen Aufwand bedeutet, alles ordentlich zu verputzen«, meint er. »Uns gefällt es so, wie es ist.«

Previous pages: *Owens lives and works in a grand building on the Place du Palais Bourbon near the French national assembly.*
Right: *A plywood and concrete daybed covered with fox fur stands in the press office.*
Below: *Owens designed the plywood and steel table in the press showroom, as well as the chairs upholstered in beaver fur. The oil painting between the windows was created by the Slovenian collective Irwin. The photo on the right is by Rick Castro.*

Pages précédentes : *Owens vit et travaille dans un superbe immeuble de la place du Palais Bourbon, près de l'Assemblée Nationale.*
À droite : *Dans le bureau de presse, un canapé en contreplaqué et béton tapissé de renard.*
En bas : *Owens a dessiné la table en contreplaqué et acier dans cette salle où les collections sont présentées à la presse. Le tableau entre les fenêtres est du collectif slovène Irwin. La photo à droite est de Rick Castro.*

Vorhergehende Seiten: *Owens lebt und arbeitet in einem prächtigen Gebäude an der Place du Palais Bourbon neben der französischen Nationalversammlung.*
Rechts: *Eine Liege aus Sperrholz und Beton, die mit Fuchsfellen bedeckt ist, steht im PR-Büro.*
Unten: *Owens entwarf den Tisch aus Sperrholz und Stahl im PR-Showroom sowie die mit Biberfellen bezogenen Stühle. Das Ölgemälde zwischen den Fenstern stammt vom slowenischen Künstlerkollektiv Irwin. Das Foto rechts ist von Rick Castro.*

Above: The ground-floor showroom in the 1950s annex with plywood and steel benches and tables.
Right: The high-backed bench upholstered in felted cashmere is another of Owens's furniture creations.
Following pages: This space on the ground floor in the annex is used as an extra office. The table and "Gallic" chairs are made from plywood. The bench on the right is upholstered in cashmere.

En haut : Des bancs et une table en acier dans le showroom du rez-de-chaussée, situé dans une annexe des années 1950.
À droite : Owens a également dessiné le banc à haut dossier tapissé en cachemire feutré.
Pages suivantes : Un espace au rez-de-chaussée qui sert également de bureau. La table et les chaises « Gallic » sont en contreplaqué. Le banc sur la droite est tapissé en cachemire.

Oben: Der Showroom im Anbau aus den 1950er-Jahren mit Bänken und Tischen aus Sperrholz und Stahlplatten.
Rechts: Die Bank mit der hohen Ummantelung und dem Bezug aus Kaschmirfilz ist ebenfalls eine von Owens' Möbelkreationen.
Folgende Seiten: Dieser Raum im Erdgeschoss des Anbaus wird als zusätzliches Büro genutzt. Der Tisch und die »Gallic«-Stühle sind aus Sperrholz. Die Bank rechts ist mit Kaschmir bezogen.

Above: *A room on one of the upper floors serves as the library. The object on the right is a totem lamp made from resin and cashmere.*
Right and facing page: *Several Owens-designed chairs in the master bathroom incorporate real antlers. The leather and goat fur boots are from his Autumn-Winter 07 "Exploder" collection. The vintage jacket is made from monkey fur.*
Following pages: *All the furnishings in the ground-floor showroom were created by Owens. They include the plywood "Antler" chair, the bronze vases on the table and the pair of "Bubble" chairs upholstered in shearling on the right.*

En haut : *Une pièce à l'étage sert de bibliothèque. L'objet à droite est une lampe totem réalisée en résine et cachemire.*
À droite et page de droite : *Pour sa chambre, Owens a créé plusieurs sièges incorporant des bois de cerfs. Les bottes en cuir et poils de chèvre font partie de la collection automne-hiver 2007, intitulée « Exploder ». La veste vintage est en singe.*
Pages suivantes : *Tout le mobilier du showroom a été dessiné par Rick Owens. Il inclut le siège « Antler » en contreplaqué, les vases en bronze sur la table et les deux chaises « Bubble » tapissées de rason.*

Oben: *Ein Zimmer im Obergeschoss dient als Bibliothek. Das Objekt rechts ist eine Totem-Lampe aus Gießharz, mit Kaschmir bezogen.*
Rechts und gegenüberliegende Seite: *Für die verschiedenen von Owens entworfenen Stühle im Bad wurden echte Geweihe verwendet. Die Stiefel aus Leder und Ziegenfell stammen aus seiner Herbst-Winter-07-Kollektion »Exploder«. Die Vintage-Jacke ist aus Affenfell.*
Folgende Seiten: *Alle Möbel im Erdgeschoss-Showroom im Anbau sind von Owens. Dazu gehören der Sperrholzstuhl »Antler«, die Bronzevasen auf dem Tisch und die beiden »Bubble«-Stühle rechts, die mit Shearling-Wolle bezogen sind.*

Facing page and left: *The vintage hoofed stool in the master bedroom was a gift from a friend. The throw on the bed is made from mink and the rugs from the fur of Chinese squirrels.*
Below: *A space on the ground floor serves as the staff kitchen.*

Page de gauche et à gauche : *Dans la chambre d'Owens, un tabouret à sabots vintage offert par un ami. Le dessus-de-lit est en vison, les tapis sont en peaux d'écureuils chinois.*
En bas : *Au rez-de-chaussée, un espace aménagé en cuisine pour les employés.*

Gegenüberliegende Seite und links: *Der alte Hocker mit Hufen im Schlafzimmer war das Geschenk eines Freundes. Der Bettüberwurf ist aus Nerz, und die Teppiche sind aus dem Fell chinesischer Eichhörnchen.*
Unten: *Ein Raum im Erdgeschoss dient als Teeküche für die Angestellten.*

Previous pages: *Behind Owens's desk is a cardboard model for a mirrored wall, which he created for a store belonging to the French luxury company Revillon.*

Pages précédentes : *Derrière le bureau d'Owens, la maquette en carton d'un mur en miroirs qu'il a créé pour Revillon, une boutique de la maison de luxe.*

Vorhergehende Seiten: *Hinter Owens' Schreibtisch steht ein Pappmodell für einen Wandspiegel, den er für einen Laden der französischen Luxusfirma Revillon entwarf.*

Decorator Alberto Pinto's clients read like a Who's Who of international society. They include Fiat heiress Marella Agnelli, financier Michel David-Weill, and the Saudi and Jordanian royal families. Pinto himself used to live in palatial surroundings – a 15-room apartment on the Quai d'Orsay. At the end of the 1990s, however, he decided to downscale and moved to a 500-square-meter space, which used to house his offices. "I felt a need for a more intimate ambience, some place warm and contemporary," he explains. Throughout, the décor reflects his signature eclectic style. There are Asian artefacts, Anglo-Indian furniture and a touch of French Art Deco. The kitchen was inspired by American movies of the 1950s, the dramatic colour in the entrance hall by legendary designer David Hicks. According to Pinto, it's the perfect way to "lend character to a potentially dull space".

Alberto Pinto

La liste des clients du décorateur Alberto Pinto ressemble à un Who's Who de la haute société internationale, incluant Marella Agnelli, le financier Michel David-Weill et les familles royales saoudienne et jordanienne. Jusqu'à la fin des années 1990, il vivait dans son propre petit palais, un appartement de quinze pièces sur le Quai d'Orsay, puis il a décidé de se réduire et d'emménager dans les 500 mètres carrés qui abritaient autrefois ses bureaux. « J'ai ressenti le besoin d'une ambiance plus intime, chaleureuse et contemporaine. » Le décor reflète son style éclectique typique : on y trouve des objets asiatiques, des meubles anglo-indiens et une touche d'Art Déco. La cuisine s'inspire des films américains des années 1950 et la couleur théâtrale de l'entrée du légendaire designer David Hicks. Selon Pinto, c'est l'idéal pour « donner du caractère à un espace a priori sans charme ».

Die Kunden des Innenarchitekten Alberto Pinto lesen sich wie das Who's Who der internationalen Society. Dazu gehören die Fiat-Erbin Marella Agnelli, der Finanzier Michel David-Weill sowie die königlichen Familien Saudi-Arabiens und Jordaniens. Pinto war ebenfalls ein Palastambiente gewöhnt – eine 15-Zimmer-Wohnung am Quai d'Orsay. Aber Ende der 1990er-Jahre beschloss er, sich zu verkleinern, und zog in eine 500 Quadratmeter große Wohnung, in der früher sein Büro untergebracht war. »Ich hatte das Bedürfnis nach einer intimeren Umgebung, nach einem warmen und zeitgenössischen Ort«, so Pinto. Die Einrichtung weist durchweg den für ihn so typischen Stil-Mix auf. Es gibt asiatisches Kunsthandwerk, anglo-indische Möbel und einen Hauch französisches Art déco. Die Küche ist von amerikanischen Filmen der 1950er-Jahre inspiriert und der dramatische Anstrich im Flur vom legendären Designer David Hicks. Laut Pinto ist das die perfekte Methode, »einem eher langweiligen Raum Charakter zu geben«.

Previous pages: In the library, a chair has been decorated with a motif inspired by Jean Cocteau. The vintage lacquer table is Chinese.
Above: The walls of the dining room are adorned with a custom hand-painted wallpaper from Gracie, representing Ottoman scenes. The 1940s screen hides the entrance to the kitchen.
Right: A view from the entrance into the guest bathroom. The chest of drawers dates from the 1930s and was created by Syrie Maugham.
Facing page: Two Serge Roche plaster torches flank an English gilt-wood sofa of c. 1860.

Pages précédentes : Dans la bibliothèque, un fauteuil italien a été re-tapissé et orné d'un motif inspiré par Jean Cocteau. La table en laque est chinoise.
En haut : Les murs de la salle à manger présentent des scènes otto-manes de chez Gracie. Le paravent des années 1940 cache l'entrée de la cuisine.
À droite : Une vue de la salle de bains des invités depuis l'entrée. La commode a été créée par Syrie Maugham dans les années 1930.
Page de droite : Deux torchères en plâtre de Serge Roche flanquent un canapé anglais en bois doré, datant de 1860 environ.

Vorhergehende Seiten: In der Bibliothek steht ein neoklassizistischer italienischer Stuhl mit einem Motiv à la Jean Cocteau. Der Lacktisch im alten Stil stammt aus China.
Oben: Die Esszimmerwände ziert eine maßgefertigte, handbemalte Tapete von Gracie, die osmanische Szenen zeigt. Der Paravent aus den 1940er-Jahren verbirgt den Eingang zur Küche.
Rechts: Ein Blick vom Flur ins Gästebad. Die Kommode ist aus den 1930er-Jahren und wurde von Syrie Maugham entworfen.
Gegenüberliegende Seite: Zwei Gipsleuchten von Serge Roche flan-kieren ein englisches Giltwood-Sofa von ca. 1860.

New Paris Interiors   Alberto Pinto

Above: The living room brings together pieces from diverse origins. The Coromandel screen is Chinese. The chests used as coffee tables are Japanese and the side table is Anglo-Indian.
Right: In the master bathroom, a portrait of the Maharani of Cooch Behar hangs above a stone console.
Facing page: A 19th-century German armchair stands next to the tub in one of the guest bathrooms.
Following pages: A checkerboard black-and-white pattern dominates the kitchen and pantry.

En haut : Le salon rassemble des meubles d'origines diverses : le paravent du XVIIIᵉ siècle en laque de Coromandel est chinois ; les coffres reconvertis en tables basses sont japonais ; le guéridon est anglo-indien.
À droite : Dans la chambre de maître, un portrait de la maharani du Cooch Behar suspendu au-dessus d'une console en pierre Art Déco.
Page de droite : Un fauteuil allemand du XIXᵉ siècle près d'une baignoire dans l'une des salles de bains des invités.
Pages suivantes : Un motif en damier noir et blanc domine la cuisine.

Oben: Im Wohnzimmer wurden Möbel verschiedener Herkunft miteinander kombiniert. Der Coromandel-Paravent stammt aus China. Die Truhen, die als Couchtische dienen, sind japanisch, und der Beistelltisch ist anglo-indischen Ursprungs.
Rechts: Im Schlafzimmer hängt ein Porträt der Maharani von Cooch Behar über einer Art-déco-Steinkonsole.
Gegenüberliegende Seite: In einem der Gästebäder steht neben der Wanne ein deutscher Sessel aus dem 19. Jahrhundert.
Folgende Seiten: Ein Schachbrettmuster beherrscht die Küche.

When Isabelle Puech and Benoît Jamin first visited this former restoration workshop for fairground rides, it hadn't been occupied for some 30 years. "It was covered in plastic sheeting and was pitch-black," recalls Jamin. Their goal, they recall, was to make it into something homely. They reconfigured the space around an internal patio and kept a wooden mezzanine and some old doors. Today, it is filled with almost as much poetry as the handbags that the pair create under the Jamin Puech label. There are chairs by Eames, Marcel Breuer and Hans Wegner, as well as the skeleton of an ostrich, a stuffed crocodile, a collection of antlers and an enormous Montblanc pen (no doubt a publicity gadget). As they say, "It's at once a cabinet of curiosities, an industrial space and somewhere that's very cosy."

Isabelle Puech & Benoît Jamin

Quand Isabelle Puech et Benoît Jamin ont découvert cet ancien atelier de restauration de manèges, il était abandonné depuis 30 ans. « Il était tapissé de bâches en plastique et il y faisait noir comme dans un four », se souvient Jamin. Pour le rendre chaleureux, ils ont reconfiguré l'espace autour d'un patio tout en conservant la mezzanine en bois et quelques vieilles portes. Aujourd'hui, le décor est aussi poétique que les sacs à main que le couple crée pour la marque Jamin Puech. Des sièges d'Eames, de Marcel Breuer et d'Hans Wegner côtoient un squelette d'autruche, un crocodile empaillé, une collection de massacres et un énorme stylo Montblanc (sans doute un gadget publicitaire). « C'est à la fois un cabinet de curiosités, un espace industriel et un nid douillet », déclarent-ils.

Als Isabelle Puech und Benoît Jamin die frühere Restaurationswerk-statt für Jahrmarktkarussells das erste Mal sahen, lag sie bereits seit mehr als 30 Jahren verlassen da. »Alles war mit Plastikfolie abge-deckt, und es war stockfinster«, erinnert sich Jamin. Ihr Ziel bestand darin, hier ein Zuhause zu schaffen. Sie gestalteten den Raum um den Innenhof neu und behielten nur die Galerie aus Holz sowie einige alte Türen bei. Heute verfügen die Räumlichkeiten über fast so viel Poesie wie die Handtaschen, die das Paar unter dem Label Jamin Puech kreiert. Es gibt Stühle von Eames, Marcel Breuer und Hans Wegner, aber auch das Skelett eines Straußvogels, ein ausgestopftes Krokodil, eine Geweihsammlung und einen riesigen Montblanc-Füller (zweifellos ein Werbegag). Beide sagen über ihr Heim: »Es ist ein Kuriositätenkabinett, Industrieloft und ein gemütliches Zuhause zugleich.«

Christian Restoin knew that he and his wife, Carine Roitfeld, would buy their apartment even before he saw it. "When I spotted the building, I felt it was for us," he recalls. "The location and the view are just fantastic." Roitfeld is the editor-in-chief of French Vogue, Restoin the former owner of the clothing company Equipment. As for the flat, it hadn't been touched since the mid-1960s. To get it into shape, they called upon English architect David Chipperfield. The idea was to create something very pure, without touching the historical features, which give the flat its spirit. The fireplaces and elaborate mouldings remained firmly in place and a hand-picked selection of design classics installed. Chipperfield also created lots of custom storage units. "I was 100% behind his every decision," asserts Restoin. "There was a great complicity between us."

Carine Roitfeld & Christian Restoin

« Quand j'ai vu l'immeuble, avec sa situation et sa vue fantastiques, j'ai su qu'on allait prendre l'appartement », se souvient Christian Restoin. Ancien propriétaire de la société de confection Equipment, il est marié à Carine Roitfeld, rédactrice en chef du Vogue français. L'appartement n'avait pas été remodelé depuis les années 1960. Pour le remettre en état, le couple a fait appel à l'architecte anglais David Chipperfield avec pour objectif de créer un espace très pur sans toucher aux détails historiques qui donnent son esprit au lieu. Les cheminées et les pâtisseries sont donc restées en place, formant un écrin à des classiques du design soigneusement choisis. Chipperfield a créé partout des unités de rangement. « Je l'ai suivi à 100% ; j'ai une grande complicité avec lui », déclare Roitfeld.

Christian Restoin wusste schon vor der Besichtigung, dass er und seine Frau Carine Roitfeld die Wohnung kaufen würden: »Als ich das Gebäude sah, spürte ich: Das ist es. Die Lage und die Aussicht sind einfach fantastisch.« Roitfeld ist Chefredakteurin der französischen Vogue und Restoin der frühere Eigentümer der Modefirma Equipment. Besagte Wohnung war seit Mitte der 1960er-Jahre nicht mehr restauriert worden. Um sie in Form zu bringen, engagierten die beiden den englischen Architekten David Chipperfield. Sie wollten etwas sehr Puristisches, ohne jedoch den historischen Charakter anzutasten, der der Wohnung ihr ganz besonderes Flair verleiht. Die Kamine und Stuckarbeiten blieben erhalten, dafür besteht die Einrichtung aus handverlesenen Designklassikern. Chipperfield schuf außerdem jede Menge Stauraum. »Ich stand zu hundert Prozent hinter jeder seiner Entscheidungen«, so Restoin. »Wir verstanden uns blind.«

Previous pages: *Roitfeld and Restoin were particularly seduced by the views from the apartment. Here, you can see the Hôtel des Invalides, with its golden dome. A suite of sofas designed by Charles Pfister for Knoll surround a Ludwig Mies van der Rohe coffee table in the sitting room.*
Right: *A view of the fireplace in the sitting room, which is flanked by a pair of Penaudio speakers.*
Below: *The sycamore storage unit was custom-designed by David Chipperfield.*

Pages précédentes : *Roitfeld et Restoin ont été particulièrement séduits par les vues depuis l'appartement. Ici, on aperçoit l'Hôtel des Invalides avec son dôme doré. Dans le salon, un ensemble de canapés dessinés par Charles Pfister pour Knoll entoure une table basse de Ludwig Mies van der Rohe.*
À droite : *La cheminée du salon, flanquée de haut-parleurs Penaudio.*
En bas : *Le meuble de rangement en sycomore a été réalisé sur mesure par David Chipperfield.*

Vorhergehende Seiten: *Roitfeld und Restoin beeindruckte besonders der Blick aus dem Appartement. Von hier aus sieht man das Hôtel des Invalides mit seiner goldenen Kuppel. Im Wohnzimmer wurden Sofas, die von Charles Pfister für Knoll entworfen wurden, um einen Couchtisch von Ludwig Mies van der Rohe gruppiert.*
Rechts: *Ein Blick auf den Kamin im Wohnzimmer, der von zwei Penaudio-Lautsprechern eingerahmt wird.*
Unten: *Das Sideboard aus Platanenholz ist eine Sonderanfertigung von David Chipperfield.*

Above and right: The dining table was originally a desk belonging to Le Corbusier. The chairs are by Ludwig Mies van der Rohe.
Following pages: Clockwise from top left: The central kitchen block is coated in a terrazzo resin. The sycamore bed was designed by Chipperfield, as was the bedhead, which doubles as a closet at the back. The curvaceous wall light is by Robert Dudley Best. Sturdy teak was chosen for the bathroom flooring. Another Chipperfield storage unit dominates the hall.

En haut et à droite : La table de salle à manger était autrefois un bureau appartenant à Le Corbusier. Les chaises sont de Ludwig Mies van der Rohe.
Pages suivantes : De gauche à droite dans le sens des aiguilles d'une montre : le bloc central de la cuisine est revêtu de terrazzo en résine. Le lit en sycomore a été conçu par Chipperfield ; la tête de lit s'ouvre par-derrière en formant un placard. L'applique flexible est de Robert Dudley Best. Pour la salle de bains, les propriétaires ont choisi un plancher solide en teck. Un autre meuble de rangement créé par Chipperfield domine l'entrée.

Oben und rechts: Der Esstisch war ursprünglich ein Schreibtisch, der Le Corbusier gehörte. Die Stühle sind ein Entwurf von Ludwig Mies van der Rohe.
Folgende Seiten: Im Uhrzeigersinn von oben links: Der zentrale Küchenblock wurde mit Terrazzogießharz beschichtet. Das Bett aus Platanenholz ist ein Entwurf von Chipperfield, genauso wie das Betthaupt, das von der anderen Seite als Schrank zu benutzen ist. Das kurvenreiche Wandlicht ist von Robert Dudley Best. Beim Badezimmerboden fiel die Wahl auf strapazierfähiges Teakholz. Ein Stauraumelement von Chipperfield entworfen, beherrscht den Flur.

Dodie Rosekrans may be the doyenne of San Francisco society. Her taste, however, is anything but traditional. "It's highly sophisticated, highly individual and not at all predictable," states decorator Hutton Wilkinson. Proof of that is evident in her Parisian pied-à-terre. Wilkinson worked on it with the late and legendary Tony Duquette. "The idea," he says, "was for it to be like a gypsy tent." They covered the walls with Mogul embroideries, created dining chairs inspired by the Peacock Throne of Shiva and lined the white awnings on the balcony with leopard skin. They also made a mirror from an antique Thai carving and glued on Burmese Buddha's eyes. "Tony used to say, 'It's the only mirror that looks back at you'," recalls Rosekrans. Wilkinson, meanwhile, remembers playfully asking a policeman who lived there. "An Indian Princess," came the reply.

Dodie Rosekrans

Dodie Rosekrans a beau être la doyenne de la haute société de San Francisco, son goût n'a rien de traditionnel. Selon son décorateur Hutton Wilkinson, « il est hautement sophistiqué, très personnel et totalement imprévisible ». Son pied-à-terre parisien en est la preuve. Wilkinson y a travaillé avec feu le légendaire Tony Duquette. « L'idée était d'en faire une tente de bohémien. » Ils ont tapissé les murs de broderies mongoles, créé des chaises inspirées du trône du Paon de Shiva et doublé les auvents en toile blanche du balcon de léopard. Ils ont aussi conçu un miroir à l'aide d'une sculpture thaï antique et collé dessus des yeux de bouddha birman. « Tony disait : C'est le seul miroir qui vous regarde en retour », se souvient Rosekrans. Wilkinson a demandé un jour à un policier qui habitait dans l'appartement. Il a répondu « une princesse indienne ».

Dodie Rosekrans kann man gut und gerne als die Doyenne der höheren Gesellschaft von San Francisco bezeichnen. Doch ihr Geschmack ist alles andere als konventionell. »Er ist hochraffiniert, sehr individuell und kein bisschen vorhersehbar«, bestätigt der Innenarchitekt Hutton Wilkinson. Das zeigt sich auch an ihrem Pariser Pied-à-terre. Wilkinson hat es gemeinsam mit dem legendären, inzwischen verstorbenen Tony Duquette eingerichtet. »Es sollte aussehen wie ein Zigeunerzelt«, sagt er. Sie bespannten die Wände mit Mogul-Stickereien, entwarfen Esszimmerstühle, die vom Pfauenthron des Shiva inspiriert sind, und bezogen die weißen Sonnensegel auf dem Balkon mit Leopardenfell. Außerdem verwandelten sie ein altes thailändisches Schnitzwerk in einen Spiegel und klebten die Augen eines burmesischen Buddhas darauf. »Tony meinte: ›Das ist der einzige Spiegel, der zurückschaut‹«, erinnert sich Rosekrans. Und Wilkinson erinnert sich noch gut daran, wie er einmal zum Spaß einen Polizisten fragte, wer dort wohne. »Eine indische Prinzessin«, lautete die Antwort.

A historian and novelist, Count Gonzague Saint Bris is the author of some 40 books and the recipient of numerous prizes, including the Prix Interallié. The son of a diplomat, he was partly raised at the family seat – Le Clos Lucé near Amboise – where Leonardo da Vinci spent the last three years of his life. His Parisian duplex has an equally rich history. Housed in one of the city's earliest neo-Renaissance town mansions, it has successively been an arms room, a painter's atelier and the venue of jazz guitarist Django Reinhardt's first concerts. With great panache, Saint Bris has furnished it as a tribute to his love of literature. There are chairs that belonged to Sir Walter Scott, the altar on which poet Alfred de Vigny was christened and a replica of the "Kiss Me Quick corner" in Victor Hugo's house on Guernsey. In Saint Bris' own words: "Every room is like a chapter and the apartment like a novel."

Gonzague Saint Bris

Historien et romancier Gonzague Saint Bris a publié plus de quarante ouvrages et reçu d'innombrables prix littéraires, dont l'Interallié. Fils de diplomate, il a grandi en partie dans le manoir familial, le Clos Lucé près d'Amboise, où Léonard de Vinci passa les trois dernières années de sa vie. Son duplex parisien a lui aussi un riche passé. Situé dans l'un des plus anciens hôtels particuliers néo-renaissance de la capitale, il fut salle d'armes puis atelier de peintre avant d'accueillir les premiers concerts du guitariste de jazz, Django Reinhardt. Avec panache, Saint Bris en a fait un hommage à son amour de la littérature. On y trouve des chaises ayant appartenu à Sir Walter Scott, l'autel sur lequel Alfred de Vigny fut baptisé et une réplique du coin « Kiss Me Quick » de la maison de Victor Hugo à Guernesey. Pour Saint Bris : « Chez moi, chaque pièce est comme un chapitre, ainsi l'appartement est un roman. »

Der Historiker und Schriftsteller Comte Gonzague Saint Bris verfasste über 40 Bücher und gewann mehrere Literaturpreise, darunter den Prix Interallié. Der Diplomatensohn wuchs zum Teil auf dem Landsitz seiner Familie – Le Clos Lucé bei Amboise – auf, wo Leonardo da Vinci die letzten drei Jahre seines Lebens verbrachte. Seine Pariser Maisonettewohnung kann auf eine ähnlich illustre Geschichte zurückblicken. Sie befindet sich in einer der frühesten Stadtvillen der Neorenaissance und war einst Waffenkammer, Künstleratelier und Veranstaltungsort für die ersten Konzerte des Jazzgitarristen Django Reinhardt. Saint Bris hat sie mit großer Opulenz eingerichtet, gewissermaßen als Hommage an seine Liebe zur Literatur. Es gibt Stühle, die einst Sir Walter Scott gehörten, den Altar, auf dem der Dichter Alfred de Vigny getauft wurde, und eine Replik der »Kiss Me Quick corner« in Victor Hugos Haus auf Guernsey. Um mit Saint Bris' eigenen Worten zu sprechen: »Bei mir ist jedes Zimmer wie ein Kapitel, die Wohnung wie ein Roman.«

Previous pages: The main room is dominated by a chandelier, from the opera house in Manaus in the middle of the Amazonian jungle in Brazil. The sculpted chairs once belonged to writer Sir Walter Scott.
Facing page: Quotations from Chopin, Mozart and Berlioz in Saint Bris' handwriting. The magnifying glass was a present from the author/photographer Maxime Du Camp to Gustave Flaubert.
Above: The bed with the canopy à la Polonaise once belonged to author George Sand.
Following pages: Clockwise from top left: Count Gonzague Saint Bris; the altar table on which poet Alfred de Vigny was christened; a portrait of La Fayette hangs on one of the two facing balconies; a suit of armour, that once belonged to Francis I. of France; Saint Bris writes on a copy of La Fayette's desk; a bust of Francis I. of France; a portrait of François René de Chateaubriand and a bust by Jean-Baptiste Carpeaux in one corner of the living room; the front door is decorated with the arms of all the owners of the Saint Bris family seat, Le Clos Lucé.

Pages précédentes : La pièce principale est dominée par un lustre provenant de l'opéra de Manaus, au milieu de la jungle amazonienne du Brésil. Les chaises sculptées appartenaient autrefois à Sir Walter Scott.
Page de gauche : Des citations de Chopin, de Mozart et de Berlioz calligraphiées par Saint Bris. La loupe était un présent de l'auteur et photographe Maxime Du Camp à Gustave Flaubert.
En haut : Le lit « à la polonaise » a appartenu à George Sand.
Pages suivantes : À partir de la gauche dans le sens des aiguilles d'une montre : Gonzague Saint Bris ; l'autel sur lequel Alfred de Vigny fut baptisé ; un portrait de La Fayette dans l'une des deux galeries se faisant face ; dans un coin du séjour, un portrait de François René de Chateaubriand et un buste signé Jean-Baptiste Carpeaux ; la porte d'entrée est ornée des armoiries de tous les propriétaires du manoir familial des Saint Bris, le Clos Lucé.

Vorhergehende Seiten: Der Salon wird von einem Kronleuchter beherrscht, der aus der Oper von Manaus, mitten im brasilianischen Amazonas-Dschungel, stammt. Die fein ziselierten Stühle gehörten einst dem Schriftsteller Sir Walter Scott.
Gegenüberliegende Seite: Zitate von Chopin, Mozart und Berlioz in Saint Bris' Handschrift. Das Vergrößerungsglas war ein Geschenk des Schriftstellers und Fotografen Maxime Du Camp an Gustave Flaubert.
Oben: Das Bett mit dem Himmel à la Polonaise gehörte einmal der Schriftstellerin George Sand.
Folgende Seiten: Im Uhrzeigersinn von oben links: Comte Gonzague Saint Bris; der Altar, auf dem der Dichter Alfred de Vigny getauft wurde; ein Porträt von La Fayette hängt in einer der beiden einander gegenüberliegenden Galerien; eine Rüstung, die einst dem französischen König Franz I. gehörte; Saint Bris schreibt an einer Kopie von La Fayettes Schreibtisch; ein Porträt von François René de Chateaubriand und eine Büste von Jean-Baptiste Carpeaux in einer Ecke des Wohnzimmers; die Vordertür schmücken Wappen aller Eigentümer des Saint-Bris-Familienlandsitzes Le Clos Lucé.

Gerald Schmorl works as a consultant to several luxury-goods houses
and lives in an apartment in the 9th arrondissement, the décor of
which he conceived as a showcase for his contemporary art collection.
The discreet colour scheme is dominated by various shades of grey.
The mix of classical elements and geometric motifs is inspired by the
late David Hicks. In the entrance hall is a traditional scenic wallpaper
by Zuber. On the dining-room walls, a swirling, graphic motif created
in situ by Swiss artist Stéphane Dafflon. And the art? It's mainly
American. Particularly striking is a gold painting with an elaborate
damask motif by New York-based artist Rudolf Stingel. Placed next to
a puristic John McCracken plank sculpture, it perfectly illustrates
Schmorl's style. As he himself says: "My taste ranges from minimalist
to very baroque".

Gerald Schmorl

Gerald Schmorl, consultant pour plusieurs maisons de luxe,
habite dans un appartement du 9ᵉ arrondissement dont le décor
sert d'écrin à sa collection d'art contemporain. Discrète, la palette
de couleurs est dominée par des nuances de gris. Le mélange
d'éléments classiques et de motifs géométriques s'inspire de feu
David Hicks. Un papier peint panoramique de Zuber vous accueille
dans l'entrée. Les murs de la salle à manger sont ornés d'arabesques
graphiques peintes in situ par l'artiste suisse, Stéphane Dafflon.
L'art, lui, est principalement américain. Parmi les œuvres les plus
frappantes, une peinture dorée à motif de brocart signée du New-
yorkais Rudolf Stingel est placée près d'une sculpture planche
puriste de John McCracken, illustrant parfaitement le style Schmorl.
Comme il le dit lui-même : « Mon goût varie d'un côté minimaliste
à un côté très baroque. »

Beruflich ist Gerald Schmorl Berater für mehrere Luxusfirmen. Privat
wohnt er im 9. Arrondissement in einem Appartement, in welchem er
seine Sammlung zeitgenössischer Kunst perfekt zur Geltung bringt.
Die zurückhaltenden Farben bestehen überwiegend aus verschiedenen
Grautönen. Die Mischung aus klassischen Elementen und geometri-
schen Motiven sind von dem verstorbenen David Hicks inspiriert. Den
Flur schmückt eine Panoramatapete von Zuber und die Esszimmerwände ein schwungvolles, grafisches Motiv, das der Schweizer Künstler
Stéphane Dafflon direkt vor Ort kreiert hat. Und die Kunst? Sie ist
überwiegend amerikanisch. Besonders beeindruckend ist ein goldenes
Gemälde mit einem opulenten Damastmotiv. Es stammt von dem in
New York lebenden Künstler Rudolf Stingel. Typisch Schmorl ist, dass
er es neben eine puristische John-McCracken-Plankenskulptur gehängt
hat. Wie sagt er so schön? »Mein Geschmack reicht von Minimalisti-
schem bis hin zu Barockem.«

Previous pages: *Scenic wallpaper by Zuber.*
Facing page: *To the left is a John Tremblay painting entitled "Silver Curtain". The ornate chandelier is 18th-century Italian.*
Above: *The living room acts as a showcase for Schmorl's collection of contemporary art. From left to right, a work by Peter Halley called "Silver Prison", a John McCracken plank sculpture entitled "Cool One" and a 2004 oil and enamel on canvas by Rudolf Stingel. The Louis XVI-style chair is from Potsdam.*
Right: *A Steven Parrino painting has been placed in front of a mirror.*

Pages précédentes : *Un papier peint panoramique de la maison Zuber.*
Page de gauche : *À gauche, une toile de John Tremblay intitulée « Silver Curtain ». Le beau lustre italien date du XVIIIᵉ siècle.*
En haut : *Le séjour sert de vitrine à la collection d'art contemporain de Schmorl. De gauche à droite, une œuvre de Peter Halley intitulée « Silver Prison », une sculpture planche de John McCracken, « Cool One », et une huile et émail sur toile de Rudolf Stingel. Le fauteuil de style Louis XVI vient de Potsdam.*
À droite : *Une œuvre de Steven Parrino placée devant un miroir.*

Vorhergehende Seiten: *Die Panoramatapete ist von Zuber.*
Gegenüberliegende Seite: *Links hängt ein Gemälde von John Tremblay mit dem Titel »Silver Curtain«. Der Kristalllüster aus dem 18. Jahrhundert stammt aus Italien.*
Oben: *Das Wohnzimmer dient als Showroom für Schmorls Sammlung zeitgenössischer Kunst. Von links nach rechts: eine Arbeit, »Silver Prison«, von Peter Halley, eine Plankenskulptur von John McCracken mit dem Titel »Cool One« und ein Werk in Öl und Lack von Rudolf Stingel aus dem Jahr 2004. Der Sessel im Louis-XVI-Stil stammt aus Potsdam.*
Rechts: *Ein Bild von Steven Parrino steht vor einem Spiegel.*

Above: Two André Arbus chairs flank an antique English mahogany
desk in Schmorl's office.
Right: Schmorl's brushed-steel-and-bronze four-poster bed dates from
the 1970s.
Facing page: The swirling motifs on the dining-room walls are the
work of Swiss artist Stéphane Dafflon. On the Eero Saarinen table
stands an 18th-century Fürstenberg porcelain urn. The stool front right
is by Carlo Mollino and the black wall sculpture by Vincent Szarek.

En haut : Dans la pièce de travail de Schmorl, deux fauteuils d'André
Arbus flanquent un vieux bureau anglais en acajou.
À droite : Le lit à baldaquin en acier brossé et bronze date des années
1970.
Page de droite : Les volutes sur les murs de la salle à manger ont
été peintes par l'artiste suisse Stéphane Dafflon. Sur la table d'Eero
Saarinen, une urne en porcelaine du XVIIIᵉ siècle de la manufacture de
Fürstenberg. Le tabouret au premier plan à droite est de Carlo Mollino
et la sculpture noire sur le mur de Vincent Szarek.

Oben: Zwei Sessel von André Arbus stehen an einem antiken englischen Mahagoni-Tisch in Schmorls Arbeitszimmer.
Rechts: Schmorls Himmelbett aus gebürstetem Stahl und Bronze
stammt aus den 1970er-Jahren.
Gegenüberliegende Seite: Das schwungvolle Motiv auf den Esszim-
merwänden ist eine Arbeit des Schweizer Künstlers Stéphane Dafflon.
Auf dem Tisch von Eero Saarinen steht eine Porzellanurne aus dem
18. Jahrhundert von Fürstenberg. Der Hocker vorne rechts ist von
Carlo Mollino und die schwarze Wandskulptur von Vincent Szarek.

New Paris Interiors   Gerald Schmorl

"I like open spaces," declares the creative director of the French edition of AD magazine, Angelica Steudel. Originally, her flat had what she calls "Parisian charm"– corridors, doors and walls everywhere. It was reconfigured with the help of interior designer Laurent Buttazzoni and now boasts but one door – a Bordeaux-coloured partition between her bedroom and bathroom. Throughout, the aesthetic is influenced by both Japan and Scandinavia. There are also a large number of Steudel's own creations – ceramics, pillows, a tablecloth made from kimono fabrics and black ink drawings. "I love black ink," she enthuses. "It's my favourite smell." Her most treasured possession, however, is the vintage Knoll sofa in the living room. "It was a wedding present to my parents," she explains. "It's the only thing I'd never give away."

Angelica Steudel

« J'aime les espaces ouverts », déclare Angelica Steudel, directrice de la création pour l'édition française de la revue AD. À l'origine, son appartement avait « un charme tout parisien », à savoir des couloirs, des portes et des murs partout. Reconfiguré avec l'aide du décorateur Laurent Buttazzoni, il ne possède plus qu'une seule cloison bordeaux entre la chambre de Steudel et sa salle de bains. L'esthétique d'ensemble est mi-japonaise, mi-scandinave. On y trouve également de nombreuses créations de la maîtresse de maison : des céramiques, des coussins, une nappe en tissus de kimono et des dessins à l'encre. « J'adore l'encre noire. C'est mon odeur favorite », dit-elle. Mais son vrai trésor, c'est le canapé Knoll vintage du séjour. « Un cadeau de mariage fait à mes parents. La seule chose que je ne donnerai jamais. »

»Ich mag offene Räume«, so Angelica Steudel, die Kreativdirektorin der französischen Ausgabe des AD-Magazins. Ursprünglich besaß ihre Wohnung, was man »Pariser Charme« nennt – überall Flure, Türen und Wände. Sie wurde mithilfe des Interiordesigners Laurent Buttazzoni umgestaltet und verfügt mittlerweile nur noch über eine Tür – eine bordeauxfarbene Schiebewand zwischen Schlafzimmer und Bad. Die gesamte Ästhetik zeigt Einflüsse aus Japan und Skandinavien. Es gibt auch viele eigene Kreationen von Steudel – Keramiken, Kissen, eine Tischdecke aus Kimono-Stoff und schwarze Tuschzeichnungen. »Ich liebe schwarze Tusche«, schwärmt sie. »Das ist mein Lieblingsduft.« Ihr kostbarster Besitz ist allerdings das Vintage-Sofa von Knoll im Wohnzimmer. »Es war ein Hochzeitsgeschenk für meine Eltern«, erzählt sie. »Das ist das Einzige, von dem ich mich niemals trennen werde.«

Previous pages: *The chair is by Harry Bertoia. The butterfly stool is by Sori Yanagi, the ceramics by Philippe Barde and Gisela Koch.*
Above: *The Knoll sofa was a wedding present to Steudel's parents. The two benches were designed by George Nelson and the occasional tables by Christian Liaigre. To the left of the fireplace is a Mats Gustafson illustration. To the right, several of Steudel's own black-ink drawings.*
Right: *The linen pillows were created by Steudel. The lamp is by Isamu Noguchi.*

Pages précédentes : *La chaise est d'Harry Bertoia. Le tabouret papillon est de Sori Yanagi, les céramiques sont de Philippe Barde et Gisela Koch.*
En haut : *Le canapé Knoll fut offert aux parents de Steudel pour leur mariage. Les deux bancs ont été dessinés par George Nelson et les tables d'appoint par Christian Liaigre. À gauche de la cheminée, une illustration de Mats Gustafson. À droite, plusieurs dessins à l'encre noire de Steudel.*
À droite : *Les oreillers en lin ont été créés par Steudel. La lampe est d'Isamu Noguchi.*

Vorhergehende Seiten: *Der Stuhl ist von Harry Bertoia. Der Schmetterlingshocker ist von Sori Yanagi, die Keramiken stammen von Philippe Barde und Gisela Koch.*
Oben: *Das Knoll-Sofa war ein Hochzeitsgeschenk für Steudels Eltern. Die beiden Bänke sind ein Entwurf von George Nelson und die Beistelltischchen von Christian Liaigre. Links vom Kamin hängt eine Zeichnung von Mats Gustafson, rechts davon stehen mehrere Tuschzeichnungen, die Steudel selbst gemacht hat.*
Rechts: *Die Leinenkissen entwarf Steudel. Die Lampe ist von Isamu Noguchi.*

Right: The chairs are by Pierre Guariche and Arne Jacobsen, the table by the latter. The kitchen unit comes from Ikea.
Below: In the office is a Zanotta desk and a traditional Japanese cabinet.

À droite : Des chaises de Pierre Guariche et d'Arne Jacobsen, autour d'une table d'Arne Jacobsen. Les éléments de cuisine viennent d'Ikea.
En bas : Dans le bureau, une table de travail Zanotta et un cabinet traditionnel japonais.

Rechts: Die Stühle sind von Pierre Guariche und Arne Jacobsen, der Tisch ist ebenfalls von Arne Jacobsen. Die Einbauküche stammt von Ikea.
Unten: Im Büro stehen ein Schreibtisch von Zanotta sowie ein traditioneller japanischer Schrank.

Facing page: Steudel created both the vase and tablecloth herself. The latter was made by sewing together Japanese kimono fabrics. On the wall is a collection of invitations to fashion shows.

Page de droite : Steudel a réalisé elle-même le vase et la nappe. Cette dernière est un patchwork de tissus de kimono. Au mur, une collection d'invitations à des défilés de mode.

Gegenüberliegende Seite: Steudel schuf sowohl die Vase als auch die Tischdecke. Letztere entstand durch das Zusammennähen mehrerer Kimono-Stoffe. An der Wand sieht man eine Sammlung von Einladungen zu Modeschauen.

Above: A pair of Japanese "geta" sandals stands outside the shower. Inside is a paving stone, which was picked up from a street on the Île Saint-Louis.
Right: A Comme des Garçons leather jacket stands on a mannequin in the corridor.

En haut : Une paire de sandales « geta » japonaises attend devant la douche. A l'intérieur de celle-ci, un pavé ramassé dans une rue de l'Île Saint-Louis.
À droite : Dans le couloir, un blouson en cuir Comme des Garçons sur un mannequin de couturière.

Oben: Ein Paar japanischer »Geta«-Sandalen steht vor der Dusche. Darin befindet sich ein Pflasterstein, der von einer Straße auf der Île Saint-Louis stammt.
Rechts: Im Flur hängt eine Lederjacke von Comme des Garçons über einer Schneiderpuppe.

New Paris Interiors Angelica Steudel

*"When I first took this apartment, it was beyond shabby chic,"
declares designer Hervé Van der Straeten. Fifteen years later and it's
simply chic. Take the sitting room with its heady but harmonious mix
of styles – a Louis XVI sofa, Danish 1960s furniture, a dramatic mobile
by artist Xavier Veilhan and many of Van der Straeten's own creations.
After starting off designing jewellery for the likes of Thierry Mugler
and Christian Lacroix, he ebbed into creating furniture and now counts
such top decorators as Peter Marino and Alberto Pinto among his
fans. His friends, meanwhile, are often invited round for dinner. Van
der Straeten created the large, open kitchen so that he can cook and
chat with them at the same time. He also kitted out the bedroom all
in red and reupholstered a pair of Le Corbusier armchairs in shocking
green satin. As he says, "It makes them more glamorous".*

Hervé Van der Straeten

« Quand j'ai pris l'appartement, il était au-delà du 'shabby chic' »,
déclare Hervé Van der Straeten. Quinze ans plus tard, il est
simplement chic. Dans son séjour au mélange de styles grisant et
harmonieux, un canapé Louis XVI, des meubles danois des années
1960 et un mobile spectaculaire de Xavier Veilhan côtoient les
créations du maître de maison. Ce dernier a retapissé une paire de
fauteuils de Le Corbusier en satin vert shocking « pour les rendre
plus glamour ». Sa chambre est rouge du sol au plafond. Après
avoir dessiné des bijoux pour Thierry Mugler et Christian Lacroix,
Van der Straeten s'est lancé dans le mobilier et compte aujourd'hui
parmi ses admirateurs de grands décorateurs tels Peter Marino et
Alberto Pinto. Comme il aime recevoir ses amis à dîner, il a créé
une grande cuisine ouverte pour pouvoir papoter tout en leur
mitonnant des petits plats.

»Als ich mich für diese Wohnung entschied, war sie jenseits von
›shabby chic‹«, meint der Designer Hervé Van der Straeten. Fünfzehn
Jahre später ist sie einfach nur chic. Da ist zum einen das Wohnzimmer mit seinem harmonischen Stil-Mix aus einem Louis-XVI-Sofa,
skandinavischen Möbeln aus den 1960er-Jahren, einem ausgefallenen
Mobile des Künstlers Xavier Veilhan und vielen Entwürfen von Van
der Straeten selbst. Nachdem er Schmuck für so große Namen wie
Thierry Mugler und Christian Lacroix entworfen hatte, verlegte sich
der Designer auf das Entwerfen von Möbeln. Heute zählt er Top-
Interior-Designer wie Peter Marino und Alberto Pinto zu seinen Fans.
Gern lädt er seine Freunde zum Abendessen ein. Van der Straeten
entwarf deshalb eine große, offene Küche, damit er gleichzeitig kochen
und sich unterhalten kann. Er kleidete das Schlafzimmer ganz in
Rot ein und ließ ein Paar Le-Corbusier-Sessel mit grellgrünem Satin
beziehen. »Das macht sie glamouröser«, so der Hausherr.

Previous pages: One of Van der Straeten's "Dada" mirrors hangs above the fireplace. The other objects are wonderfully eclectic. Among them, Xavier Veilhan's "Petit Mobile", red plaster columns from the 1930s and one of the designer's "Mondrian" coffee tables.
Facing page: Both the "Miroir Solaire" mirror and the "Franges" cabinet in the entry corridor were created by Van der Straeten.
Above: The standing lamp between the windows is by Isamu Noguchi.
Right: The all-red bedroom features Pierre Paulin's "Orange Slice Chair" and one of Van der Straeten's "Capsule" stools.

Pages précédentes : Un des miroirs « Dada » de Van der Straeten au-dessus de la cheminée du séjour. Parmi la collection merveilleusement éclectique d'objets : un « Petit Mobile » de Xavier Veilhan, des colonnes en plâtre rouge des années 1930, un canapé du XVIIIe siècle et une des tables basses « Mondrian » dessinées par le maître de maison.
Page de gauche : Le « Miroir Solaire » et le cabinet « Franges » dans l'entrée sont des créations de Van der Straeten.
En haut : Le lampadaire entre les fenêtres est d'Isamu Noguchi.
À droite : Dans la chambre rouge, un fauteuil « Orange Slice » de Pierre Paulin et un des tabourets « Capsule » de Van der Straeten.

Vorhergehende Seiten: Einer von Van der Straetens »Dada«-Spiegeln hängt über dem Kamin im Wohnzimmer. Auch die anderen Objekte sind wunderbar eklektisch. Dazu gehören Xavier Veilhans »Petit Mobile«, rote Gipssäulen aus den 1930er-Jahren, ein Sofa aus dem 18. Jahrhundert sowie einer der »Mondrian«-Couchtische des Designers.
Gegenüberliegende Seite: Sowohl der »Miroir Solaire«-Spiegel als auch der »Franges«-Schrank im Flur sind von Van der Straeten.
Oben: Die Stehlampe zwischen den Fenstern ist von Isamu Noguchi.
Rechts: Im Schlafzimmer stehen Pierre Paulins »Orange Slice«-Stuhl und einer von Van der Straetens »Capsule«-Hockern.

Art dealers and collectors Cathy and Paolo Vedovi originally planned to redecorate their Parisian pied-à-terre themselves. That is until Cathy stopped by the Parisian gallery of interior designer Chahan Minassian. "Everything there was so perfect," recalls the co-founder of the Galerie Emmanuel Perrotin in Miami. "I said to myself, I'll never manage to do something like that." Within 15 minutes, she'd bought a coffee table, two side tables and various lamps and ceramics. She had also hired Minassian for the project. Inspiration came from a photo of the swimming pool of the Ruhl Palace in Marrakesh. The motif of the tiles was copied for the living room rug and the dining room fitted out with three turquoise tables and a banquette, which Minassian refers to as "a stretched chair". The whole process apparently went swimmingly, too. As Vedovi says, "It was as if someone had waved a magic wand!"

Cathy & Paolo Vedovi

Marchands et collectionneurs d'art, Cathy et Paolo Vedovi comptaient initialement décorer eux-mêmes leur pied-à-terre parisien. Puis Cathy est passée à la galerie du décorateur Chahan Minassian. « Tout y était tellement parfait. Je me suis dit que je n'arriverai jamais à faire quelque chose comme ça. » Un quart d'heure plus tard, elle en ressortait avec une table basse, deux consoles, plusieurs lampes et céramiques, et avait engagé Minassian. Elle s'inspira d'une photo de la piscine du palais Ruhl à Marrakech. Le motif de son carrelage fut copié pour le tapis du salon et la salle à manger fut aménagée avec trois tables turquoise et une banquette que Minassian qualifie de « chaise étirée ». Depuis, les Vedovi se sentent comme des poissons dans l'eau dans leur nouveau décor. Comme dit Cathy : « C'était comme si quelqu'un avait agité une baguette magique. »

Ursprünglich wollten die Kunsthändler und Sammler Cathy und Paolo Vedovi ihr Pariser Pied-à-terre selbst neu einrichten. Aber das war, bevor Cathy an der Pariser Galerie des Interiordesigners Chahan Minassian vorbeiging. »Dort war einfach alles perfekt«, erinnert sich die Mitbegründerin der Galerie Emmanuel Perrotin in Miami. »Ich dachte, so was kriegst du nie selbst hin.« Innerhalb einer Viertelstunde kaufte sie einen Couchtisch, zwei Beistelltischchen und verschiedene Lampen und Keramiken. Außerdem heuerte sie Minassian für das Projekt an. Als Inspiration diente ein Foto des Pools im Palais Ruhl in Marrakesch. Das Fliesenmotiv wurde für den Wohnzimmerteppich entlehnt, während man das Esszimmer mit drei türkisen Tischchen und einer Bank bestückte, die Minassian als »extrem langen Sessel« bezeichnet. Der Einrichtungsprozess ging wie von selbst. Wie sagt Vedovi noch so schön? »Es war, als habe jemand den Zauberstab geschwungen!«

Previous pages: A work by René Magritte entitled "Shéhérazade" hangs in one corner of the sitting room.
Facing page: Three Chinese-style ceramic stools stand on a Bedouin rug from Morocco. The painting is by Bernard Frize.
Above: In the entrance hall is a Plexiglas and brushed steel table by Maria Pergay. The bronze sculpture is by Germaine Richier.
Right: Mike Kelley's dog is made from painted black velvet on wood. The glass ball was created by the Japanese artist Ritsue Mishima.

Pages précédentes : Dans un coin du séjour, une œuvre de René Magritte intitulée « Shéhérazade ».
Page de gauche : Les trois tabourets en céramique d'inspiration chinoise sont posés sur un tapis bédouin marocain. Le tableau est de Bernard Frize de la Galerie Emmanuel Perrotin.
En haut : Dans le hall d'entrée, une table en Plexiglas et acier brossé de Maria Pergay. La sculpture en bronze est de Germaine Richier.
À droite : Le chien de Mike Kelley est en velours noir peint collé sur bois. La boule en verre est une œuvre de la Japonaise Ritsue Mishima.

Vorhergehende Seiten: Eine Arbeit von René Magritte mit dem Titel »Shéhérazade« hängt in einer Ecke des Wohnzimmers.
Gegenüberliegende Seite: Drei Keramikhocker im China-Stil stehen auf einem Beduinenteppich aus Marokko. Das Gemälde ist von Bernard Frize aus der Galerie Emmanuel Perrotin.
Oben: Blickfang im Flur ist ein Tisch aus Plexiglas und Stahl von Maria Pergay. Die Bronzeskulptur ist von Germaine Richier.
Rechts: Mike Kelleys Hund besteht aus schwarzem Samt auf Holz. Die Glaskugel ist von der japanischen Künstlerin Ritsue Mishima.

Previous pages: Two imposing Vladimir Kagan sofas and a Salviati glass chandelier dominate the living room. In the far corner is Takashi Murakami's "Kinoko Isu" sculpture, made from fibreglass, steel and acrylic paint.
Above: On the right is a large oil painting by Peter Doig. The rug was custom made by David Hicks.
Right: A 1950s ceramic lamp stands on a desk created by a student of Gio Ponti.

Pages précédentes : Deux imposants canapés de Vladimir Kagan et un lustre en verre Salviati dominent le séjour. Au fond, une sculpture de Takashi Murakami, « Kinoko Isu », en fibre de verre, acier et peinture acrylique.
En haut : À droite, une huile de Peter Doig. Le tapis a été réalisé sur mesure par David Hicks.
À droite : Une lampe des années 1950 en céramique posée sur un bureau créé par un élève de Gio Ponti.

Vorhergehende Seiten: Zwei imposante Vladimir-Kagan-Sofas und ein Glaslüster von Salviati beherrschen das Wohnzimmer. Im Hintergrund sieht man Takashi Murakamis Skulptur »Kinoko Isu« aus Fiberglas, Stahl und Acrylfarbe.
Oben: Rechts hängt ein großes Ölgemälde von Peter Doig. Der Teppich ist eine Sonderanfertigung von David Hicks.
Rechts: Eine Keramiklampe aus den 1950er-Jahren steht auf einem Schreibtisch, der von einem Schüler Gio Pontis entworfen wurde.

Right: In one corner of the living room hangs Jean-Michel Othoniel's "Black is Beautiful", from the Galerie Emmanuel Perrotin.
Below: The glass and granite coffee table was created by the Brazilian designer Amaury Cardoso. The two paintings on the mantle are from Murakami's "Dokuro" series.
Following pages: In the dining room, a Curtis Jere bronze tree and a set of 19th-century Japanese vases stand on an inlaid chest of drawers. The artwork is by Jonathan Meese. In the sitting room, a Gamboni vase and sculptures by Ken Stetert and Germaine Richier stand in front of a Christopher Wool painting.

À droite : Dans un coin du séjour, une œuvre de Jean-Michel Othoniel, « Black is Beautiful », provenant de la Galerie Emmanuel Perrotin.
En bas : La table basse en verre et granit a été crée par le designer brésilien Amaury Cardoso. Les deux tableaux sur le manteau de la cheminée appartiennent à la série Dokuro de Murakami.
Pages suivantes : Dans la salle à manger, un arbre en bronze de Curtis Jere et une paire de vases japonais du XIXᵉ siècle posés sur une commode en marqueterie. Le tableau est de Jonathan Meese. Dans le petit salon, un vase de Gamboni ainsi que des sculptures de Ken Stetert et de Germaine Richier devant une toile de Christopher Wool.

Rechts: In einer Ecke des Wohnzimmers hängt Jean-Michel Othoniels »Black is Beautiful« aus der Galerie Emmanuel Perrotin.
Unten: Der Couchtisch aus Glas und Granit ist ein Entwurf des brasilianischen Designers Amaury Cardoso. Die beiden Bilder auf dem Kaminsims stammen aus der »Dokuro«-Serie von Murakami.
Folgende Seiten: Im Esszimmer stehen ein Bronzebaum von Curtis Jere sowie ein Set japanischer Vasen aus dem 19. Jahrhundert auf einer mit Intarsien verzierten Schubladenkommode. Das Bild ist von Jonathan Meese. Im Wohnzimmer stehen eine Gamboni-Vase und Skulpturen von Ken Stetert und Germaine Richier vor einem Gemälde von Christopher Wool.

Facing page: Two Chahan Minassian banquettes, a silver artwork by Rudolf Stingel and an embroidery by Alighiero Boetti.
Above: A Roger Tallon staircase leads from the kitchen to the roof terrace. The Paola Pivi piece "Untitled" on the wall is made from pearls.
Right: Next to the master bed is a Karl Springer snakeskin lamp and a 1940s Lucite chair upholstered with ocelot fur.
Following pages: The terrace offers spectacular views of the Grand Palais and the Eiffel Tower.

Page de gauche : Les deux banquettes ont été dessinées par Chahan Minassian. Le tableau en argent est de Rudolf Stingel et la broderie « De uno a cento e vice versa » d'Alighiero Boetti.
En haut : Un escalier de Roger Tallon relie la cuisine à la terrasse sur le toit. L'œuvre en perles sans titre sur le mur est de Paola Pivi.
À droite : Près du lit dans la chambre principale, une lampe en peau de serpent de Karl Springer et un fauteuil tapissé d'ocelot.
Pages suivantes : De la terrasse, on a des vues spectaculaires.

Gegenüberliegende Seite: Die beiden Liegen sind Entwürfe von Chahan Minassian, das silberne Bild stammt von Rudolf Stingel, und die Stickerei »De uno a cento e vice versa« ist von Alighiero Boetti.
Oben: Eine Wendeltreppe von Roger Tallon führt von der Küche auf den Dachgarten. Die Arbeit an der Wand von Paola Pivi besteht aus Perlen.
Rechts: Neben dem großen Bett stehen eine Lampe von Karl Springer und ein Plexiglas-Sessel aus den 1940er-Jahren mit Ozelotfellbezug.
Folgende Seiten: Die Dachterrasse bietet eine fantastische Aussicht auf den Grand Palais und den Eiffelturm.

Ask architect Joseph Dirand about this apartment created for an American TV producer and he talks in philosophical terms. He claims that he wanted to make something very abstract, "a sort of contemplative attitude" and "a very sculptural space". He also wanted to create "beauty with the least amount of effects". He worked with just two colours – black and white – and handpicked the rare furnishings (the Christian Liaigre sofas, the André Arbus dining table, the Serge Mouille lamp …). He also discreetly integrated hi-tech throughout. An extractor fan pops up from the kitchen range, a television screen drops down in front of a window and all the sockets are hidden in the floor. The only real ornament is to be found in one of the bathrooms, with its elaborate chandelier and Venetian mirror. "For me," he says, "it represents the negative image of the rest of the flat."

WDL Apartment

Quand on interroge l'architecte Joseph Dirand sur cet appartement réalisé pour un producteur de télévision américain, il répond, philosophe, qu'il a voulu créer quelque chose de très abstrait, « une sorte d'attitude contemplative », « un espace très sculptural » et « de la beauté avec un minimum d'effets ». Il n'a travaillé qu'en noir et blanc et sélectionné minutieusement le mobilier dépouillé (les canapés Christian Liaigre, la table d'André Arbus, la lampe de Serge Mouille…). L'équipement high-tech a été discrètement incorporé. Une hotte sort du bloc cuisine, un écran de télévision descend devant une fenêtre et toutes les prises sont dissimulées dans le sol. Les seuls véritables ornements sont le lustre en cristal et le miroir vénitien de la salle de bains. Selon Dirand, « elle est comme le négatif du reste de l'appartement ».

Fragt man den Architekten Joseph Dirand nach diesem Appartement, das er für einen amerikanischen Fernsehproduzenten entworfen hat, wird er philosophisch. Er sagt, er habe etwas sehr Abstraktes erzeugen wollen, »eine Art kontemplative Haltung« und »einen Raum wie eine Skulptur«. Er wollte auch »mit den geringstmöglichen Mitteln Schönheit erschaffen«. Dabei arbeitete er ausschließlich mit zwei Farben – mit Schwarz und Weiß – und suchte die wenigen Möbel (Sofas von Christian Liaigre, den Esstisch von André Arbus, die Lampe von Serge Mouille …) selbst aus. Außerdem integrierte er überall diskret jede Menge Hightech. Es gibt eine ausfahrbare Dunstabzugshaube, einen Fernsehbildschirm, der vor einem der Fenster herabgelassen werden kann, und jede Menge im Boden versteckte Steckdosen. Verspielt ist nur das Bad mit dem prächtigen Kristalllüster und dem venezianischen Spiegel. »Für mich reflektiert das sozusagen das Abwesende in der übrigen Wohnung«, so der Architekt.

Addresses / Adresses / Adressen

RUE DES BELLES-FEUILLES
Christian Baquiast
(Architect)
18, cité Trévise
75009 Paris
phone: +33 6 07 43 41 44
christian.baquiast@neuf.fr

Hugues Peuvergne
(Landscape architect)
42 bis, avenue du Général Leclerc
77400 Lagny-sur-Marne
phone: +33 1 64 30 61 75
hugues.peuvergne@wanadoo.fr

MARIA BONNAFOUS-BOUCHER
Valérie Mazérat
(Interior designer)
4, rue Saint-Nicolas
75012 Paris
phone: +33 1 43 47 32 96
valerie.mazerat@90online.fr

BERTRAND BURGALAT
Tricatel
www.tricatel.com

LES BUTTES-CHAUMONT
Sébastien Segers
(Architect)
19, rue Béranger
75003 Paris
phone: +33 1 42 72 12 09
studio@sebastiensegers.com
www.sebastiensegers.com

MICHAEL COORENGEL & JEAN-PIERRE CALVAGRAC
Coorengel & Calvagrac
(Interior designers)
43, rue de l'Echiquier
75010 Paris
contact@coorengel-calvagrac.com
www.coorengel-calvagrac.com

ALEXANDRE DE BETAK
Bureau Betak
199 Lafayette Street
New York, NY 10012
phone: +1 212 274 0669
bbcontact@bureaubetak.com
www.bureaubetak.com

FRANCK DELMARCELLE
Et Caetera
(Antique dealer)
40, rue de Poitou
75003 Paris
phone: +33 1 42 71 37 11
franckdelmarcelle@yahoo.fr
www.franckdelmarcelle.com

JEAN-LOUIS DENIOT
(Interior designer)
39, rue de Verneuil
75007 Paris
phone: +33 1 45 44 04 65
www.deniot.fr

SIMON DE PURY
Phillips de Pury & Company
(Auctioneers)
28, rue Michel Le Comte
75003 Paris
phone: +33 6 85 53 92 03

Headquarter
450 West 15 Street
New York, NY 10011
phone: +1 212 940 1200
www.phillipsdepury.com

COMTE & COMTESSE HUBERT D'ORNANO
Sisley (Cosmetics)
16, avenue George V
75008 Paris
phone: +33 1 49 52 35 00
www.sisley-cosmetics.com

ALDA FENDI
Fendi
(Fashion, leather goods & accessoiries)
24, rue François 1er
75008 Paris
phone: +33 1 49 52 84 52
www.fendi.it

ELIANE FIÉVET
(Paper designer)
3, rue du 29 Juillet
75001 Paris
phone: +33 1 42 60 68 40
eliane.fievet@club-internet.fr

DIDIER GOMEZ
Didier Gomez Interior Design D.G.I.D.
(Interior designer)
28, boulevard de Bonne Nouvelle
75010 Paris
phone: +33 1 44 61 04 00
dgidgabriel@yahoo.fr
www.didiergomez.com

MICHELLE & YVES HALARD
phone: +33 1 43 29 40 44
yves.halard@orange.fr

ANNE VALÉRIE HASH
(Fashion designer)
36, boulevard de Bonne Nouvelle
75010 Paris
phone: +33 1 48 87 97 41
www.anne-valerie-hash.com

Isabelle Stanislas
(Architect)
SO-AN
7, rue d'Aboukir
75002 Paris
phone: +33 1 44 82 62 00
info@so-an.fr
www.so-an.fr

BOULEVARD HAUSSMANN
Décoration Jacques Garcia
(Interior designer)
212, rue de Rivoli
75001 Paris
phone: +33 1 42 97 48 70
info@decojacquesgarcia.com
www.decojacquesgarcia.com

RUE JACOB
Cristina Finucci
Studio Finucci
Via Montevideo 5
00198 Roma
phone: +39 06 841 2286
studio@finucci.com
www.studiofinucci.com

PATRICIA & PHILIPPE JOUSSE
Jousse Entreprise
Mobilier d'architectes
18, rue de Seine
75006 Paris
phone: +33 1 53 82 13 60

Mobilier d'artistes et de designers 60', 70'
34, rue Louise Weiss
75013 Paris
phone: +33 1 45 83 62 48

Art contemporain
24, rue Louise Weiss
75013 Paris
phone: +33 1 53 82 10 18
infos@jousse-entreprise.com
www.jousse-entreprise.com

Emmanuel Combarel & Dominique Marrec
(Architects)
7, passage Turquetil
75011 Paris
phone: +33 1 44 93 20 60
ecdm@combarel-marrec.com
www.combarel-marrec.com

CLÉMENCE & DIDIER KRZENTOWSKI
Galerie Kreo
(Design gallery)
22, rue Duchefdelaville
75013 Paris
phone: +33 1 53 60 18 42
kreogal@wanadoo.fr
www.galeriekreo.com

HUBERT LE GALL
(Designer)
22, rue Tourlaque
75018 Paris
hubertlegall@free.fr

NATHALIE LÉTÉ & THOMAS FOUGEIROL
Nathalie Lété
(Designer)
phone: +33 1 49 60 84 76
nathalie@nathalie-lete.com
www.nathalie-lete.com

Astier de Villatte
173, rue Saint-Honoré
75001 Paris
phone: +33 1 42 60 74 13
www.astierdevillatte.com

Thomas Fougeirol
(Painter)
fougeirol.thomas@wanadoo.fr

CHRISTIAN LIAIGRE
(Interior designer)
Showroom
42, rue du Bac
75007 Paris
phone: +33 1 53 63 33 66

Showroom
61, rue de Varenne
75007 Paris
phone: +33 1 47 53 78 76
sales@christian-liaigre.fr
www.christian-liaigre.fr

CHRISTIAN LOUBOUTIN
(Shoe designer)

Shop
19, rue Jean-Jacques Rousseau
75001 Paris
phone: +33 1 42 36 05 31

Shop
38–40, rue de Grenelle
75007 Paris
phone: +33 1 42 22 33 07
www.christianlouboutin.fr

INDIA MAHDAVI
(Architect)
Showroom
3, rue las Cases
75007 Paris
phone: +33 1 45 55 67 67
showroom@indiamahdavi.com
www.indiamahdavi.com

SEAN MCEVOY
(Architect)
7, rue Gabriel Laumain
75010 Paris
phone: +33 6 61 97 26 17
mcevoy_sean@yahoo.fr

FRÉDÉRIC MÉCHICHE
(Decorator)
4, rue de Thorigny
75003 Paris
phone: +33 1 42 78 78 28

RICK OWENS & MICHÈLE LAMY
Boutique Rick Owens
(Fashion designer)
Jardins du Palais Royal
130–133, Galerie de Valois
75001 Paris
phone: +33 1 40 20 42 52
store@rickowens.eu
www.rickowens.eu

ALBERTO PINTO
(Decorator & interior designer)
Hôtel de la Victoire
11, rue d'Aboukir
75002 Paris
phone: +33 1 40 13 00 00
contact@albertopinto.com
www.albertopinto.com

ISABELLE PUECH & BENOÎT JAMIN
Jamin Puech
Boutique
26, rue Cambon
75001 Paris
phone: +33 1 40 20 40 28

68, rue Vieille du Temple
75003 Paris
phone: +33 1 48 87 84 87

43, rue Madame
75006 Paris
phone: +33 1 45 48 14 85

61, rue d'Hauteville
75010 Paris
phone: +33 1 40 22 08 32
www.jamin-puech.com

CARINE ROITFELD & CHRISTIAN RESTOIN
David Chipperfield Architects
Cobham Mews
Agar Grove, Camden

London NW1 9SB
phone: +44 20 7267 9422
info@davidchipperfield.co.uk
www.davidchipperfield.co.uk

DODIE ROSEKRANS
Tony Duquette & Hutton Wilkinson
(Decorators)
Tony Duquette Inc.
PO Box 69858
West Hollywood, CA 90069
phone: +1 310 271 4688
huttonwilkinson@hotmail.com
www.huttonwilkinson.com
www.tonyduquette.com

GERALD SCHMORL
(Designer)
schmorl@free.fr

ANGELICA STEUDEL
Buttazzoni & Associés
(Interior designer)
83, avenue Kléber
75016 Paris
phone: +33 1 40 09 98 49

HERVÉ VAN DER STRAETEN
Galerie Van der Straeten
(Design gallery)
11, rue Ferdinand Duval
75004 Paris
phone: +33 1 42 78 99 99
fax: +33 1 42 78 99 90

CATHY & PAOLO VEDOVI
Chahan Gallery
12, rue de Beaune
75007 Paris
phone: +33 1 42 96 88 88
gallery@chahan.com
www.chahan.com

Galerie Emmanuel Perrotin
76, rue de Turenne
75003 Paris
phone: +33 1 42 16 79 79
infoparis@galerieperrotin.com
www.galerieperrotin.com

194 NW 30th Street
Miami, FL 33127
phone: +1 305 573 2130
infomiami@galerieperrotin.com

GALERIE VEDOVI
69, rue du Faubourg Saint-Honoré
75008 Paris
phone: +33 1 44 51 91 76
info@galleryvedovi.com
www.galleryvedovi.com

WDL APARTMENT
Joseph Dirand Architecture
4, cour Saint-Pierre
75017 Paris
phone: +33 1 44 69 04 80
jd@josephdirand.com
www.josephdirandarchitecture.com